THE ULTIMATE FOOTBALL
ACTIVITY BOOK

Crosswords, Word Searches, Puzzles, Fun Facts,
Trivia Challenges and Much More for Football Lovers!

KURT TAYLOR

CONTENTS

INTRODUCTION

The roots of American football are largely assumed to be concentrated with the universities of the East Coast. However, the rule basis for what we call American football began in the late 19th century with Walter Camp, now known as the "Father of American Football." As one would assume given the similarities, the sport evolved from rugby's invasion of East Coast schools, though it was the local athletics clubs that ended up becoming the first to popularize the game in the United States.

The first professional football player was William "Pudge" Heffelfinger, who was paid $500 to play for the Alleghany Athletic Association in 1892. Less than a decade later, the Morgan Athletic Club formed a team on the south side of Chicago. That team changed names a few times after its 1899 creation, though many of you will know them as the Arizona Cardinals. The NFL's predecessor, the American Professional Football Association, was created in 1920 with the Racine Cardinals among the founding members, along with the Decatur Staleys and Canton Bulldogs among other smaller teams, many of whom didn't make it to the end of the season.

The following year, the Green Bay Packers joined the league and by 1922, the APFA became known as the National Football League. Among the other changes that year was the Decatur Staleys becoming the Chicago Bears. The New York Giants joined the league in 1925, and the NFL has not really looked back, expanding and contracting to its current 32-team structure. Much of the information above is unknown to the diehard fans because football was not the popular sport it is today. So much of the history is just forgotten because the roots of the NFL are normally traced to the 1960's with its competition and the AFL.

Yet everything from 1892 until the end of the 2021 season is up for grabs in the forthcoming pages. We will test you on everything from the fundamentals of football to NFL history and the legendary names written in the record book. The point of this book isn't to trick you or stump you, rather it gives you a fun way to reinforce what you do know and perhaps add a few new kernels of knowledge as well.

Now if you actually read the introduction, the first puzzle is going to be a breeze. But most of all, have some fun with these puzzles and enjoy the experience of learning more about your favorite sport.

CHAPTER

1

FIRST DOWN
General Knowledge

The Basics
THE ORIGIN STORY

We're going to test your knowledge of the earliest days of football. For each statement, select True or False and enter the corresponding letter on the appropriate line below. You'll know you have it correct when the answer to the final question is spelled out.

1. Walter Camp, the Father of American Football, was the head coach at Stanford after leaving Yale.

FACT:	C	FICTION:	P

   FACT circled, C circled

2. The first completely professional football team was created in the 20th century in Pittsburgh, Pennsylvania.

FACT:	E	FICTION:	A

   FICTION circled, A circled

3. The first professional football player was paid $500 to play in a game, and sealed his team's win with a 35-yard fumble recovery for a touchdown.

FACT:	R	FICTION:	C

   FACT circled, R circled

4. Christy Matthewson played fullback in a professional football game.

FACT:	D	FICTION:	K

   FACT circled, D circled

5. The forward pass was legalized after Jim Thorpe became a professional football player.

FACT:	E	FICTION:	I

   FICTION circled, I circled

6. The touchdown was always worth more points than a field goal.

FACT:	R	FICTION:	N

   FICTION circled, N circled

7. The New York Giants were one of the original NFL franchises to start the league in 1920.

FACT:	L	FICTION:	A

   FICTION circled, A circled

8. Chicago hosted the first indoor NFL playoff game in 1932 at Chicago Stadium.

FACT:	L	FICTION:	T

   FACT circled, L circled

9. The Lions and Packers played in the first NFL game broadcast to a national audience.

FACT:	P	FICTION:	S

   FICTION circled, S circled

What is the oldest NFL franchise still in the league?

C A R D I N A L S
1 2 3 4 5 6 7 8 9

FLAG ON THE PLAY

Dash from the end zones to pick up the flag in this field of mazes.

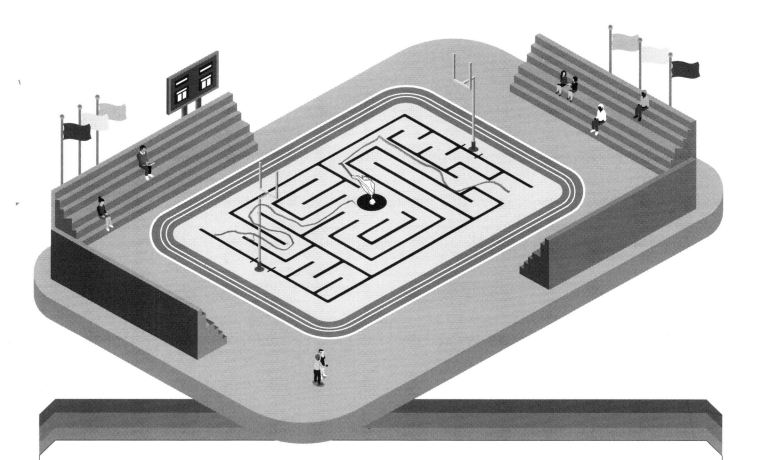

In 1941, the head coach at what is now Youngstown State University had an issue. His players would stop every time they heard the horn that signified there was a penalty on the play even though the action was still ongoing. All he wanted was a silent signal that would alert everyone to the infraction without interrupting the play.

Youngstown coach Dwight Beede tasked his wife, Irma, with creating the first flags after the coach at Oklahoma City University agreed to use the flags in a game. The first penalty flags ended up being red and white, the colors of Youngstown State, and used to negate a 17-yard touchdown for Youngstown on that October night.

Most of the referees threw away the flags after that game, telling Beede it was a bad idea, but Jack McPhee kept his flag and set about promoting it at all of the games he officiated over the next few years. By 1948, the flag was standard equipment for all officials, and the rest as they say is history.

BE THE REF

How well do you know the hand signals referees use to signify what is happening on the field. Identify each signal with the correct penalty or procedure and write it on the space provided.

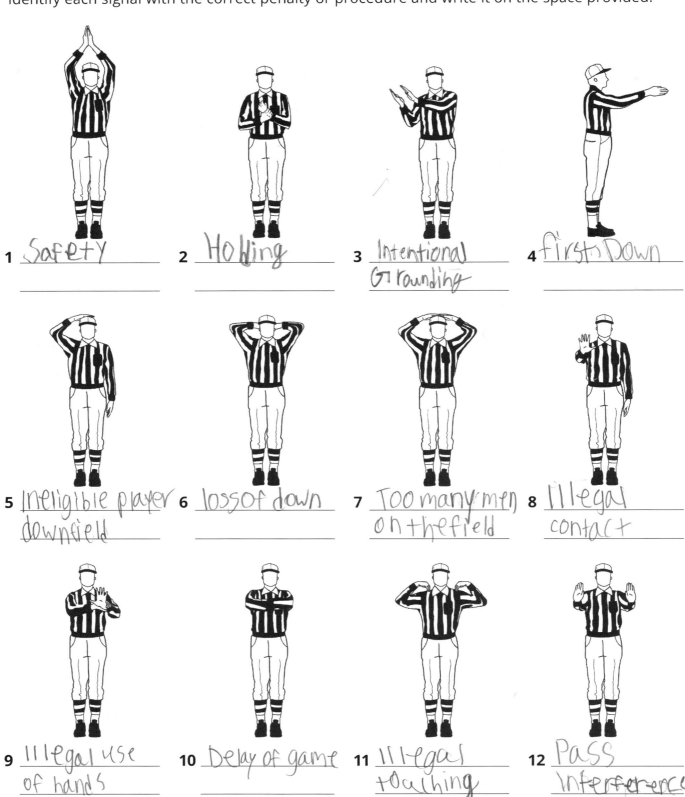

1 Safety

2 Holding

3 Intentional Grounding

4 First Down

5 Ineligible player downfield

6 loss of down

7 Too many men on the field

8 Illegal contact

9 Illegal use of hands

10 Delay of game

11 Illegal touching

12 Pass Interference

READY POSITION

Football is all about formations, and the variety of ways coaches can use the talent on the field. Can you identify each of the positions based on the basic formation we've drawn for you?

1	Center	5	Full Back
2	Half Back	6	tight end
3	Off. tackle	7	QB
4	Wide Recever	8	Off. Guard

9	Def. End	12	Inside linebacker
10	Def. takle	13	Corner back
11	Outside linebacker	14	safety

FIND THE TERM

```
M  J  B  G  Y  F  R  G  N  T  I  I  W  N  E  Q  R
E  W  F  L  K  J  W  C  U  K  N  Q  O  M  B  G  X
M  L  B  L  T  P  O  O  C  U  U  I  I  E  D  U  I
O  K  P  J  F  V  E  O  G  N  T  T  Z  E  H  G  E
T  S  L  S  E  M  L  T  S  A  E  T  F  U  S  N  V
I  O  I  R  I  C  O  A  M  M  I  E  D  L  P  O  V
O  F  A  T  Y  H  N  R  I  L  N  D  O  O  E  I  T
N  G  U  A  S  T  O  R  B  S  L  C  T  N  C  T  N
E  T  L  M  H  F  P  O  E  E  W  A  R  G  I  P  U
H  P  U  E  B  P  Z  I  K  T  I  N  O  S  A  E  O
O  J  M  N  M  L  X  F  G  J  J  T  P  N  L  C  C
L  D  M  N  V  Y  E  C  S  S  I  O  H  A  T  R  P
D  S  L  E  G  B  I  E  V  J  K  N  Y  P  E  E  A
E  S  T  H  G  I  R  P  U  A  N  I  B  P  A  T  N
R  I  N  O  I  T  E  L  P  M  O  C  N  E  M  N  S
W  E  G  A  M  M  I  R  C  S  N  S  O  R  S  I  U
Q  E  S  N  E  F  F  O  K  C  I  K  W  C  Y  D  E
```

Anthem	Fumble	Offense	Snap Count
Blitz	Holder	Pigskin	Special Teams
Canton	Huddle	Play	Timeout
Completion	Interception	Clock	Trophy
Coverage	Kickoff	Primetime	Uprights
Defense	Long Snapper	Scrimmage	
Formation	Motion	Shotgun	

WHAT'S IN A NAME?

Each clue in this crossword will hint to you how a certain NFL team earned its name.

Across

2. Company that founded the team

5. Nickname of the city's mayor

8. Famous historic event in the region

11. Honors the role the region played in US History

12. Copied name of city's baseball team

13. A color, not a bird

Down

1. Original team owner

3. The city's well-known industry

4. Scandinavian roots in the state

6. A famous poem

7. Wanted to rhyme with the local baseball team

9. Popular jazz song

10. Alma mater of team's first general manager

RAINBOW CONNECTION

Anyone can describe a team's colors using basic terms like dark blue or light red. Some teams, though, use some unique terms to describe their colors. Your job here is to identify which color palette belongs to which team.

1. Battle Red and Liberty White

2. Powder Blue and Sunshine Gold

3. Honolulu Blue

4. Aqua

5. Midnight Green

6. Old Gold

7. Pewter

8. Wolf Grey and Action Green

9. Royal and Sol

LOGO DESCRIPTIONS

Can you match our description of each logo to the team whose logo we are describing?

1. A black and red bird drawn to look like the letter "F"

2. A stampeding mammal with a red streak through its body

3. A pirate flag with a sword for the handle

4. A blue horseshoe

5. A blue five-pointed star with a white border

6. A man with an eyepatch and two swords crossing behind his head

7. A bull with its face painted half red and half blue, with a white stripe down the center and a star for an eye.

8. A tiger-striped letter "B"

9. A man in a tri-corner hat

10. An orange "C" on a navy background

11. A white horse with an orange mane

12. An orange helmet

13. An arrowhead with two letters representing the team's home city

14. A purple bird with the letter "B" on its head

15. A flaming pendant with the letter "T" and three stars surrounding the letter

16. Two white block letters representing the team's home city

A. Giants _16_

B. Patriots _9_

C. Bills _2_

D. Colts _4_

E. Broncos _11 or 2_

F. Texans _7_

G. Raiders _6_

H. Chiefs _13_

I. Ravens _14_

J. Titans _15_

K. Bears _10_

L. Falcons _falcon_

M. Bengals _8_

N. Browns _12_

O. Cowboys _5_

P. Buccaneers _3_

LARGE AND IN CHARGE

It's hard to believe there have just been five commissioners since the NFL began. So much has happened since the position was created in 1941, but just who was in charge for all of these historic moments? Identify which commissioner accomplished each milestone for the league.

1. Added anti-gambling rules into league constitution

A. Elmer Layden   **B.** Bert Bell   **C.** Pete Rozelle   **D.** Paul Tagliabue   **E.** Roger Goodell

2. Proposed and sold Monday Night Football to ABC

A. Elmer Layden   **B.** Bert Bell   **C.** Pete Rozelle   **D.** Paul Tagliabue   **E.** Roger Goodell

3. Mandated the playing of the national anthem at games

A. Elmer Layden   **B.** Bert Bell   **C.** Pete Rozelle   **D.** Paul Tagliabue   **E.** Roger Goodell

4. Shut down NFL Europe

A. Elmer Layden   **B.** Bert Bell   **C.** Pete Rozelle   **D.** Paul Tagliabue   **E.** Roger Goodell

5. Orchestrated merger with AFL

A. Elmer Layden   **B.** Bert Bell   **C.** Pete Rozelle   **D.** Paul Tagliabue   **E.** Roger Goodell

6. Created the Pro Bowl

A. Elmer Layden   **B.** Bert Bell   **C.** Pete Rozelle   **D.** Paul Tagliabue   **E.** Roger Goodell

7. The first regular-season game is played outside the United States

A. Elmer Layden   **B.** Bert Bell   **C.** Pete Rozelle   **D.** Paul Tagliabue   **E.** Roger Goodell

8. Introduced Personal Conduct Policy

A. Elmer Layden   **B.** Bert Bell   **C.** Pete Rozelle   **D.** Paul Tagliabue   **E.** Roger Goodell

9. The NFLPA is formed and negotiates for the first time with owners

A. Elmer Layden   **B.** Bert Bell   **C.** Pete Rozelle   **D.** Paul Tagliabue   **E.** Roger Goodell

10. The last time the NFL added an expansion franchise

A. Elmer Layden   **B.** Bert Bell   **C.** Pete Rozelle   **D.** Paul Tagliabue   **E.** Roger Goodell

NOT FOR LONG LEAGUE

If you've been around the NFL long enough, you'll have heard that NFL actually stands for "Not For Long." There have been a lot of swings and misses when it comes to the NFL Draft, but every once in a while, a player catches on with a team that didn't actually draft him. So in this puzzle, you have to remember which team actually drafted these players.

1. Reggie White

A. Dallas Cowboys   B. San Francisco 49ers   C. Arizona Cardinals   **D.** Philadelphia Eagles

2. Cris Carter

A. New York Jets   **B.** Philadelphia Eagles   C. Chicago Bears   D. Denver Broncos

3. Brett Favre

A. Atlanta Falcons   B. Kansas City Chiefs   C. New Orleans Saints   D. San Francisco 49ers

4. Marshall Faulk

A. Detroit Lions   B. Tampa Bay Buccaneers   **C.** Indianapolis Colts   D. Cleveland Browns

5. Curtis Martin

A. New England Patriots   B. Miami Dolphins   C. Seattle Seahawks   D. Cincinnati Bengals

6. Champ Bailey

A. Baltimore Ravens   **B.** Washington Redskins   C. Miami Dolphins   D. Dallas Cowboys

7. Shaun Alexander

A. Dallas Cowboys   **B.** Seattle Seahawks   C. Oakland Raiders   D. Kansas City Chiefs

8. Jared Allen

A. Kansas City Chiefs   B. Detroit Lions   C. Philadelphia Eagles   D. Atlanta Falcons

9. Eli Manning

A. Carolina Panthers   B. New York Jets   C. Indianapolis Colts   **D.** San Diego Chargers

10. Greg Olsen

A. New Orleans Saints   B. New York Giants   **C.** Chicago Bears   D. Seattle Seahawks

The History
EXPANDING THE FOOTPRINT

The NFL has obviously gone through a lot of changes between its founding and the modern day. Although many of the early teams ended up folding, the league has consistently grown over the last five decades into the 32-team behemoth it is today. Yet can you remember exactly when each team was added to the hallowed roster of franchises?

1. The New York Giants are the oldest non-charter member of the NFL

FACT:	C	FICTION:	I

2. The Pittsburgh Steelers and Philadelphia Eagles joined the league in the same year.

FACT:	N	FICTION:	L

3. The Dallas Cowboys are the youngest franchise in the NFC East.

FACT:	D	FICTION:	E

4. The New Orleans Saints predate the Atlanta Falcons by one season.

FACT:	V	FICTION:	I

5. The Miami Dolphins were a charter member of the American Football League.

FACT:	E	FICTION:	A

6. The NFL did not expand for 25 years after its merger with the AFL.

FACT:	L	FICTION:	N

7. The Baltimore Ravens are the last expansion franchise to not have an expansion draft.

FACT:	A	FICTION:	I

8. The Carolina Panthers and Jacksonville Jaguars joined the league in 1996.

FACT:	N	FICTION:	P

9. The Cleveland Browns did hold an expansion draft despite not technically being considered an expansion franchise.

FACT:	O	FICTION:	D

10. The Houston Texans are the only franchise to join the league in the 21st century.

FACT:	L	FICTION:	A

11. None of the teams in the NFC joined the NFL as part of a merger with another league.

FACT:	E	FICTION:	I

12. No city in California has never had an expansion team awarded to it.

FACT:	S	FICTION:	D

The last expansion franchise to relocate as of 2022.

| 1 | 2 | 3 | 4 | 5 | 6 | 7 | 8 | 9 | 10 | 11 | 12 |

THE MOVING COMPANY

Teams move around all the time, but can you identify which franchises made the following moves?

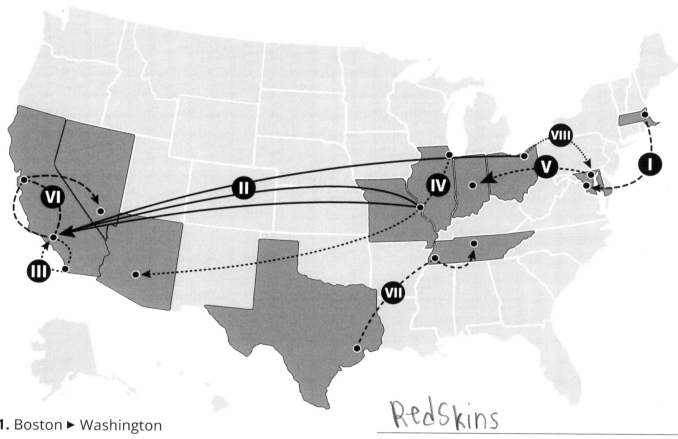

1. Boston ▶ Washington

2. Cleveland ▶ Los Angeles ▶ St. Louis ▶ Los Angeles

3. Los Angeles ▶ San Diego ▶ Los Angeles

4. Chicago ▶ St. Louis ▶ Phoenix

5. Baltimore ▶ Indianapolis

6. Oakland ▶ Los Angeles ▶ Oakland ▶ Las Vegas

7. Houston ▶ Memphis ▶ Nashville

8. Cleveland ▶ Baltimore

Redskins
Rams
Chargers
cardinals
colts
Raiders
Titans
Ravens

X'S AND O'S

Unscramble the names of these famous head coaches.

1. MLREVVYA

_____

2. RALUBPNOW

_____

3. UYMAELULABRC

_____

4. LANODTRMY

_____

5. LIBLWSAHL

_____

6. BIEICLDVRNOAM

_____

7. CCHOLKNLU

_____

8. BRUTNADG

_____

9. JDNNDOHAME

_____

10. BLLLSRCEIPLA

_____

11. HDANSOUL

_____

12. TSRAAKNHM

_____

13. CLBILEHIKICBL

_____

14. OSLMEFOTR

_____

15. AAGEORSLEGH

_____

ROAMING THE SIDELINES

Every once in a while, a coach will say something that will make you scratch your head. Yet it is those memorable quotes that oftentimes outlive their speakers, so can you match these legendary quotes with the coach who delivered them?

1. "The superior man blames himself. The inferior man blames others."

_____

2. "If they want you to cook the dinner, at least they ought to let you shop for some of the groceries."

_____

3. "That's the great thing about sports. You play to win. You play to win the game."

_____

4. "Winning isn't everything, it's the only thing."

_____

5. "They were who we thought they were. ... We played them in the third game, everybody played three quarters, the Bears are who we thought they were. That's why we took the damn field. ... They are who we thought they were! And we let them off the hook."

_____

6. "Nobody who ever gave his best regretted it."

_____

7. "The first year we knocked on the door. This year we beat on the door. Next year we're gonna kick the son of a b---- in."

_____

8. "Playoffs? Don't talk about - playoffs? You kidding me? Playoffs? I just hope we can win a game."

_____

9. "When it's too tough for them, it's just right for us."

_____

10. "We're onto Cincinnati."

_____

THE FOOLISH CLUB

When a group of businessmen got together to start a rival football league to the NFL, everyone figured they were crazy. Yet more than 50 years after merging with the NFL, those original eight owners of the American Football League franchises are having the last laugh. Only two of the eight members of the notorious "Foolish Club" still have heirs that own their franchise, but their impact on the game is honored by their brave effort to stand up to the NFL in 1960. Match the owner to his team.

1. Bob Howsam	**A.** Raiders
2. Bud Adams	**B.** Patriots
3. Barron Hilton	**C.** Bills
4. F. Wayne Valley	**D.** Chargers
5. Ralph Wilson Jr.	**E.** Broncos
6. Harry Wismer	**F.** Jets
7. Lamar Hunt	**G.** Titans
8. Billy Sullivan	**H.** Chiefs

RAINING MONEY

The value of an NFL franchise has skyrocketed with five of the last six teams to be sold attracting at least $1 billion. Some of the earliest investors in their respective franchises are now sitting on a mountain of cash after paying pennies on the dollar for the rights to the team. Your mission here is to determine if the current owners paid more or less than the listed price for the franchise.

		LESS	MORE
1.	Daniel Snyder: $700 million		
2.	Hunt Family: $50,000		
3.	Robert Kraft: $100 million		
4.	Ford Family: $2.5 million		
5.	Rooney Family: $2,000		
6.	Glazer Family: $200 million		
7.	Halas Family: $5,000		
8.	Jerry Jones: $100 million		
9.	Arthur Blank: $500 million		
10.	Irsay Family: $20 million		

THAT'S WHAT THEY CALL ME

Some of the best athletes in sports history have iconic nicknames that are also attached to them. The NFL is no exception, with both individuals and teams earning legendary monikers, and this quiz is designed to test your knowledge of those nicknames.

1. What color was the Minnesota Vikings defense that was nicked named the "People Eaters"?

A. Pink **B.** Purple **C.** Gold **D.** Green

2. Most people know the name Red Grange, but what was his actual first name?

A. Elmer **B.** David **C.** Harris **D.** Harold

3. The St. Louis Rams and Pittsburgh Steelers rode Jerome Bettis to a lot of success, which might be how he earned what nickname?

A. The Carriage **B.** The Tricycle **C.** The Bus **D.** The Trolley

4. Elroy Hirsch had an unusual running style, earning him which nickname en route to a Hall-of-Fame career?

A. The Jockey **B.** Sidestepper **C.** Crazylegs **D.** Ducky

5. Jack Tatum never killed anyone (thankfully), but what nickname of his might convince someone otherwise?

A. The Assassin **B.** The Butcher **C.** The Guillotine **D.** The Ninja

6. In the 1980's, the Jets defensive line earned what nickname for their ferocious pass rush?

A. Blitzes over Broadway **B.** Sacks Fifth Avenue **C.** The Empire State Brigade **D.** New York Sack Exchange

7. Which prolific return man earned the nickname, "The Human Joystick"?

A. Dante Hall **B.** Josh Cribbs **C.** Devin Hester **D.** Eric Metcalf

8. We give you permission to do the Ickey Shuffle if you can tell us, what was Ickey Woods' first name?

A. Elbert **B.** Isaac **C.** Ellington **D.** Irving

9. Several NFL players have animal-themed nicknames, but which one of these is not an actual NFL moniker?

A. Honey Badger **B.** Bear Claws **C.** Muscle Hamster **D.** Bambi

10. When a team is doing poorly, sometimes their fans devise some unfortunate nicknames. Which of these monikers was never given to a losing franchise?

A. The Dolts **B.** The Aints **C.** The Bungles **D.** The Toxins

LEGENDS OF THE GAME

```
H W O F E L Z Y M L M G C T M D B
L X Y T I W P Y R P A Y T O N J J
K C D C Y W F Y B A Y Q S M S I G
G S W I N S L O W A T C Z R L Y U
R G U B G A D R W S C E E H C O R
J I U K G P P L O R Y L T C M M
M H C B T H E S P L A E D G S J J
U N Q E K U B T T S Y T D T N Q Z
E V M S U F B A O U O A R N Q I X
G N I N N A M U M O D A T T A Y S
W N S U I U C B L K H F Y M G S L
O O J U T L I A I A T P O W R B C
O C G L A K E C N Q A N E Y A H
D A N O S U D H S V T V T J H K R
S E A H L B Z F O A C F I O A N R
O D J A M G J W N X K B H D M R R
N B X E E O X A E X Y S W Z Q X B
```

Woodson   Staubach   Manning

Winslow   Singletary Graham

White   Sayers   Faulk

Unitas   Sanders   Elway

Tomlinson Rice   Deacon

Taylor   Payton   Butkus

Strahan   Montana

THE SPECIAL TEAM

Special teams is an important element of the sport, but it is often relegated as unimportant by so many fans. That is, until their favorite team misses a kick or scores a return touchdown, then it lives up to its billing as part of the three facets of the sport. We want to show our specialists lots of love by asking you about how much you really know about your punters, kickers and return men.

1. No kicker has ever successfully converted at least 90 percent of their field goals in a career.

FACT:	S	FICTION:	J

2. The NFL record for punts in a game is 16, set by the Raiders' Leo Araguz.

FACT:	E	FICTION:	H

3. Robert Bailey is the only player in league history to return a punt more than 100 yards.

FACT:	F	FICTION:	A

4. No one has successfully made every field-goal attempt in a season with at least 30 kicks attempted.

FACT:	N	FICTION:	F

5. Allen Rossum holds the record for most kickoff return yards in a career.

FACT:	E	FICTION:	F

6. The longest record punt came in 1969 when Steve O'Neal sent a 98-yard punt to the other side of the field.

FACT:	E	FICTION:	L

7. Herman Weaver had a rough season in 1978 when he set the NFL record by having six punts blocked in a season.

FACT:	E	FICTION:	A

8. Devin Hester never returned two punts for a touchdown in the same game.

FACT:	G	FICTION:	C

9. Adam Vinatieri holds the record for most point-after-attempts made in a career.

FACT:	H	FICTION:	L

10. No one has successfully made 600 field goals in their career.

FACT:	E	FICTION:	N

11. Adam Vinatieri holds the record with 44 consecutive field goal attempts made.

FACT:	S	FICTION:	R

Who holds the record for most career punts?

_____ _____ _____ _____   _____ _____ _____ _____ _____   _____ _____
1   2   3   4   5   6   7   8   9   10   11

CHAPTER

2

SECOND DOWN
American Football Conference

AFC East Hunt

D K C W L E S Z O W A O K G U T S
C I H X Y T M Z P X O H C J Z T T
S Y I I H G I Q G U W V Q N N O E S
O G F M A R I N O D B Y U I G S J
N K W M O Q K R X B B S R L Y T Q
K D I C S X P S I U L T C L J A X
A N Z D Q F H K F W A E L P E V F
S A Z Q O U L F E P Q E D R T E K
N L L J L E A O B S K C E S S R R
I G E A V L S L L E C R A P O D O
H N E Y O R L O B D L M V A R E Y
P E N N I N G T O N B I I P G O W
L W M S U Y T X K J L F C Z B E E
O E P L B H M X B R A D Y H A Y N
D N M L N C F I L F I P G G I D V
Z W T I H P S G H K G H X Y Q C U
I B K B C N P E R F E C T I O N K

Belichick	~~Jets~~	Parcells
~~Bills~~	~~Kelly~~	Patriots
Bledsoe	Levy	~~Pennington~~
~~Brady~~	Marino	~~Perfection~~
Buffalo	~~Miami~~	Shula
Csonka	~~New England~~	Testaverde
Dolphins	~~New York~~	

KNOW YOUR DRAFT: AFC EAST

1. In which round were the Dolphins able to pluck an undersized Zach Thomas out of Texas Tech?

A. 5th
B. 6th
C. 7th
D. 8th

2. Unaware of who they had uncovered, the Bills let this seventh-round selection leave on his way to being named to the Hall of Fame's all-decade team for the 1980s and 1990s.

A. Morten Andersen
B. Mike Horan
C. Gary Andersen
D. Reggie McElroy

3. Which critical part of their Super Bowl-winning offensive line did the Jets draft in the 12th round of the 1967 NFL Draft?

A. John Schmitt
B. Randy Rasmussen
C. Dave Herman
D. Winston Hill

4. The 1996 draft was great for New England as the Patriots drafted all but which one of these players that year?

A. Lawyer Milloy
B. Tedy Bruschi
C. Terry Glenn
D. Ty Law

5. After being a 24th-round pick in 1963, this quarterback won all four starts with Buffalo before finding his footing out west.

A. Roman Gabriel
B. Marlin Briscoe
C. Daryle LaMonica
D. John Hadl

6. He never actually played for the team, but Miami drafted which future MVP in the 1971 draft?

A. Brian Sipe
B. Joe Theismann
C. Mark Moseley
D. Ken Anderson

7. One of two Patriots draft picks with at least 50 career interceptions, this defensive back was a fifth-round pick in 2003.

A. Asante Samuel
B. Eugene Wilson
C. Ellis Hobbs
D. Randall Gay

8. Which backfield stalwart did the Jets pick up in the sixth round of the 1966 draft?

A. Emerson Boozer
B. Bill Mathis
C. Lee White
D. Matt Snell

9. The heart and soul of the playoff-drought era, in which round did the Bills end up selecting Kyle Williams?

A. 4th
B. 5th
C. 6th
D. 7th

10. Definitely undervalued coming out of Georgia, in which round were the Jets able to scoop up linebacker Mo Lewis?

A. 9th
B. 7th
C. 5th
D. 3rd

11. In the seventh round of the 2009 draft, the Patriots drafted which little-known quarterback out of Kent State?

A. Rob Gronkowski
B. Danny Amendola
C. Julian Edelman
D. Wes Welker

12. This receiver has caught more touchdowns than any other Dolphins draft pick despite being an eighth-round selection.

A. Mark Clayton
B. Nat Moore
C. Chris Chambers
D. O.J. McDuffie

BUFFALO BILLS JERSEY MATH

We know everyone hates math, but we think we found a way to make it fun. Simply follow the instructions and come out with the correct number or player being hinted at.

1. In his Hall of Fame speech, Andre Reed claimed six was the answer to him being added to Jim Kelly. In reality, it's this Bills legend who survived the playoff drought.

   _____

2. Multiply Tyrod Taylor with Jack Kemp, then tack on an extra point to reach this five-time Pro Bowl nose tackle who earned those honors by a nose.

   _____

3. Taking Fred Jackson away from Butch Byrd, you are left with this running back who ranks fourth in team history in rushing yards.

   _____

4. Adding together Josh Allen and Eric Moulds results in the number this man wore during the Bills' Super Bowl run.

   _____

5. No one can wear triple digits at the moment, but if you start at the century mark and lop off Scott Norwood, you'd find this special teams ace who was pretty close to perfection.

   _____

6. Subtracting Micah Hyde from Phil Hansen results with this All-Pro center who was the pivot for the Bills' four Super Bowl squads.

   _____

7. Brian Moorman is added to Thurman Thomas, then doubled to reach this number worn by Scott Chandler.

   _____

8. Triple Tre White, then subtract Steve Christie to find this longtime Bills offensive lineman who was named a Pro Bowler in his final eight seasons in Buffalo.

   _____

9. Start with Aaron Schobel, then take away Darryl Talley to get this Buffalo legend who served both as a ball-hawking defensive back and the Bills' radio commentator.

   _____

10. When Henry Jones is subtracted from longtime offensive lineman Jim Ritcher, it results in this safety who flew all around the field for the Bills for five seasons.

   _____

HISTORY OF THE BUFFALO BILLS

1. Which longtime Bills kicker is the team's all-time leading scorer with 1,011 points?

A. Tyler Bass   **B.** Scott Norwood   **C.** Rian Lindell   **D.** Steve Christie

2. Who is the only quarterback besides Josh Allen to throw for 4,000 yards in a season for Buffalo?

A. Drew Bledsoe   **B.** Jim Kelly   **C.** Joe Ferguson   **D.** Ryan Fitzpatrick

3. Who has scored the most rushing touchdowns in Bills history?

A. O.J. Simpson   **B.** Thurman Thomas   **C.** Cookie Gilchrist   **D.** Fred Jackson

4. Who holds Buffalo's single-season record for receiving yards in a season?

A. Lee Evans   **B.** Stefon Diggs   **C.** Andre Reed   **D.** Eric Moulds

5. Many talented Bills receivers have caught 10 touchdown passes in a season, but who is the only person to catch 11 in a year for Buffalo?

A. Bill Brooks   **B.** Stevie Johnson   **C.** Elbert Dubenion   **D.** Peerless Price

6. Who holds the Bills record for most career interceptions with 40 in his career?

A. Tony Greene   **B.** Charles Rome   **C.** Butch Byrd   **D.** Mark Kelso

7. Whose 4.5 sacks in a game against Carolina is the franchise record?

A. Aaron Schobel   **B.** Bruce Smith   **C.** Bryce Paup   **D.** Mario Williams

8. What is the Bills record for most points scored in a single game?

A. 49   **B.** 52   **C.** 58   **D.** 63

9. How big was Buffalo's record-setting comeback in 1993 against Houston?

A. 32 points   **B.** 30 points   **C.** 28 points   **D.** 26 points

10. Who did the Bills thump 42-0 in the most lopsided win in team history?

A. Arizona Cardinals   **B.** Cleveland Browns   **C.** Indianapolis Colts   **D.** Seattle Seahawks

MIAMI DOLPHINS 3 & OUT

Can you spot the odd-man out? Three of these answers actually answer the prompt, so your job is to spot the outlier.

1. Never named Walter Payton Man of the Year

A. Dan Marino   **B.** Jason Taylor   **C.** Mike Pouncey   **D.** Dwight Stephenson

2. Played at least 12 seasons with the Dolphins

A. Richmond Webb   **B.** Bob Griese   **C.** Nat Moore   **D.** Bob Kuechenberg

3. Threw for 300 yards in a game for the Dolphins

A. Cleo Lemon   **B.** Gus Frerotte   **C.** Brock Osweiler   **D.** Matt Moore

4. Never caught 10 passes in a game for Miami

A. Oronde Gadsden   **B.** Mark Duper   **C.** Nat Moore   **D.** Duriel Harris

5. Named NFL Defensive Player of the Year by the Associated Press

A. Jason Taylor   **B.** Zach Thomas   **C.** Doug Betters   **D.** Dick Anderson

6. Never returned multiple kickoffs and multiple punts for a touchdown with the Dolphins

A. Jakeem Grant   **B.** Mercury Morris   **C.** Ted Ginn Jr.   **D.** Freddie Solomon

7. Did not win a game as Miami's starting quarterback

A. Tyler Thigpen   **B.** Sage Rosenfels   **C.** Rick Norton   **D.** Trent Green

8. Ran for 200 yards in a game for the Dolphins

A. Reggie Bush   **B.** Jay Ajayi   **C.** Ronnie Brown   **D.** Lamar Smith

9. Coached the Dolphins in a playoff game

A. Joe Philbin   **B.** Dave Wannstedt   **C.** Adam Gase   **D.** Tony Sparano

10. Has their jersey number retired by the team

A. Bob Griese   **B.** Larry Little   **C.** Larry Csonka   **D.** Dan Marino

HISTORY OF THE MIAMI DOLPHINS

1. Which Dolphins kicker is the team's all-time leading scorer at more than 1,000 points?

A. Olindo Mare   **B.** Garo Yepremian   **C.** Pete Stoyanovic   **D.** Jason Sanders

2. Which of these Dolphins passing records is not held by Dan Marino?

A. Yards, career   **B.** Completions, season   **C.** Yards, season   **D.** Yards, game

3. Who holds the Dolphins record for rushing yards in a season?

A. Jay Ajayi   **B.** Larry Csonka   **C.** Ronnie Brown   **D.** Ricky Williams

4. Who holds Miami's record in career receiving yards?

A. Chris Chambers   **B.** Mark Duper   **C.** Nat Moore   **D.** Mark Clayton

5. Which receiver became the first Dolphins receiver to catch 100 passes and eventually set the team record with 112 receptions in a season?

A. Tony Nathan   **B.** Chris Chambers   **C.** Jarvis Landry   **D.** O.J. McDuffie

6. How many interceptions did Jake Scott have in six seasons with the Dolphins to set the franchise's career record?

A. 35   **B.** 37   **C.** 39   **D.** 42

7. Whose team record did Jason Taylor tie when he finished with 18.5 sacks in 2002?

A. Bob Baumhower   **B.** Vern Den Herder   **C.** Doug Betters   **D.** Bill Stanfill

8. What is the Dolphins record for most points scored in a game, set in 1977 against the Rams?

A. 51   **B.** 55   **C.** 59   **D.** 64

9. How long was Miami's drive in 2012 against the Jets that took nearly 12 ½ minutes off the clock while marching 94 yards?

A. 19 plays   **B.** 21 plays   **C.** 24 plays   **D.** 25 plays

10. Who did the Dolphins shellack 52-0 in 1972 for the most lopsided win in team history?

A. Kansas City Chiefs   **B.** Baltimore Colts   **C.** New England Patriots   **D.** New York Jets

NEW YORK JETS ALMA MATERS

Match the player with where he played his final season of college football before jumping to the NFL.

1. Mo Lewis	**A.** Temple
2. Don Maynard	**B.** Arizona State
3. Joe Namath	**C.** Pittsburgh
4. D'Brickashaw Ferguson	**D.** Maryland Eastern Shore
5. Mark Gastineau	**E.** South Carolina
6. Curtis Martin	**F.** Alabama
7. Freeman McNeil	**G.** UC-Davis
8. Ken O'Brien	**H.** Marshall
9. Wayne Chrebet	**I.** UCLA
10. Emerson Boozer	**J.** Hofstra
11. Chad Pennington	**K.** Georgia
12. John Abraham	**L.** Virginia
13. Aaron Glenn	**M.** UTEP
14. Wesley Walker	**N.** Texas A&M
15. Joe Klecko	**O.** California

HISTORY OF THE NEW YORK JETS

1. Who holds the Jets scoring record with nearly 1,500 points?

A. Don Maynard   **B.** Jim Turner   **C.** Pat Leahy   **D.** Nick Folk

2. Who is the only single-season 4,000-yard passer in Jets history?

A. Joe Namath   **B.** Vinny Testaverde   **C.** Ken O'Brien   **D.** Chad Pennington

3. Who is the only running back in Jets history to average at least 100 yards per game in a season?

A. Freeman McNeil   **B.** Matt Snell   **C.** Curtis Martin   **D.** Emerson Boozer

4. Who holds New York's record for most receptions in a career?

A. Al Toon   **B.** Wayne Chrebet   **C.** Wesley Walker   **D.** Don Maynard

5. Which receiver is the only player to gain at least 1,500 receiving yards in a season for the Jets?

A. Santana Moss   **B.** Laveranues Coles   **C.** Al Toon   **D.** Brandon Marshall

6. Who holds the Jets record with 34 career interceptions with the team?

A. Dainard Paulson   **B.** Bill Baird   **C.** Darrelle Revis   **D.** Victor Green

7. How many sacks did Mark Gastineau record in 1984 to set the team record?

A. 21   **B.** 22   **C.** 22.5   **D.** 23.5

8. How large was New York's biggest comeback in team history on that Monday night in 2000?

A. 17 points   **B.** 21 points   **C.** 23 points   **D.** 27 points

9. Who is the only team the Jets have played at least 20 times against which they have a winning record?

A. Miami Dolphins   **B.** Cincinnati Bengals   **C.** Cleveland Browns   **D.** Buffalo Bills

10. How many points did the Jets score on Tampa Bay in 1985 for the most points in franchise history?

A. 62   **B.** 59   **C.** 57   **D.** 53

NEW ENGLAND PATRIOTS FAST FACTS

Across

4. Town where Gillette Stadium is located

6. Head coach when Patriots played first NFL game

9. Last player to be named Offensive Rookie of the Year

11. Only person ever to wear number 20 for the Patriots

12. Starting quarterback in Patriots' first Super Bowl appearance

Down

1. Scored first touchdown for Patriots in a Super Bowl

2. City where Patriots completed the 28-3 Super Bowl comeback

3. Original owner of the Boston Patriots

5. First Patriots player inducted into Pro Football Hall of Fame

7. Only player not named Tom Brady to be voted to 10 Pro Bowls

8. Name of current Patriots Mascot

10. Last non-special teams player to be named first-team All-Pro

HISTORY OF THE NEW ENGLAND PATRIOTS

1. Who is the Patriots' all-time leading scorer?

A. Gino Cappelletti **B.** Stephen Gostkowski **C.** Adam Vinatieri **D.** Tom Brady

2. In which year did Tom Brady set the Patriots' single-season record for passing yards?

A. 2011 **B.** 2012 **C.** 2013 **D.** 2014

3. Who is the Patriots' all-time leading rusher?

A. Corey Dillon **B.** Jim Nance **C.** Curtis Martin **D.** Sam Cunningham

4. Who holds the New England record with 80 career touchdowns?

A. Julian Edelman **B.** Kevin Faulk **C.** Rob Gronkowski **D.** Stanley Morgan

5. Who is the only Patriots receiver to top 1,500 yards in a season?

A. Wes Welker **B.** Randy Moss **C.** Troy Brown **D.** Julian Edelman

6. Ty Law is tied for the record with 36 interceptions, but how many of those did he return for touchdowns to set that franchise record?

A. 6 **B.** 5 **C.** 4 **D.** 7

7. Who leads the Patriots in career sacks with 100 exactly?

A. Julius Adams **B.** Andre Tippett **C.** Tedy Bruschi **D.** Willie McGinest

8. We all know about 28-3, but what is the largest regular-season comeback in team history?

A. 21 points **B.** 22 points **C.** 23 points **D.** 24 points

9. On October 18, 2009, the Patriots set multiple team records by scoring their most points in a quarter, half and game en route to the largest win in team history. How many points did they score on the Titans that day?

A. 54 **B.** 56 **C.** 57 **D.** 59

10. The Patriots also rolled to a then-record 619 yards against Tennessee in 2009, but against which opponent did New England eclipse that mark two years later with 622 total yards?

A. Miami Dolphins **B.** Buffalo Bills **C.** New York Jets **D.** Tennessee Titans

AFC North Hunt

```
I H P U L S S G M D F E D R E E D
R G O W N S R E G H P C X C J S B
Z R L W L O X E G C J K A O L J I
R U A F S K S U L W N M X W T C L
E B M R L X A A L E B Q S H C C L
G S A D A B X P I A E D X E I L I
R T L O R Y Q K L S B T G R R E C
E T U A Z C L T T D E Y S S B V B
B I H O L O I E P E O K W V R E T
S P R W N M L N W R A S O K A L N
I S E Y O T J M C I Q M A C D A R
L L P R B U U G K I S Q A W S N M
H A E Z R N F E D Y N O F H H C H
T G B Y O D F L C J F N A R A Z P
E N K Z W F B T H L G B A S W R U
O E R M N V Z N X G Y Q Y T Y Y G
R B I D S R A V E N S A Q W I W K
```

Baltimore	Cowher	Pittsburgh
Bengals	Ed Reed	Polamalu
Billick	Esiason	Ravens
Bradshaw	Graham	Ray Lewis
Browns	Harbaugh	Roethlisberger
Cincinnati	Kosar	Steelers
Cleveland	Munoz	

KNOW YOUR DRAFT: AFC NORTH

1. Which of these running backs was not drafted in the sixth round or later by the Browns?

A. Greg Pruitt   **B.** Earnest Byner   **C.** Leroy Kelly   **D.** Charlie Harraway

2. In 2015, the Ravens were able to snag this Pro Bowl tight end in the sixth round.

A. Mark Andrews   **B.** Darren Waller   **C.** Travis Kelce   **D.** George Kittle

3. In which year did the Bengals hit the jackpot by drafting both Chad Johnson and T.J. Houshmandzadeh?

A. 1999   **B.** 2002   **C.** 2000   **D.** 2001

4. The 1974 NFL Draft was famous for the Steelers drafting four Hall-of-Famers in the first five rounds. Which one of them was not picked within the first 100 picks of the draft?

A. Mike Webster   **B.** John Stallworth   **C.** Lynn Swann   **D.** Jack Lambert

5. The Steelers drafted this future Hall-of-Fame quarterback, but he threw just 17 passes for the franchise.

A. Don Meredith   **B.** Len Dawson   **C.** Johnny Unitas   **D.** Sonny Jurgenson

6. Cincinnati stayed patient and found this gem in the seventh round of the 1969 draft.

A. Fred Willis   **B.** Ken Riley   **C.** Lemar Parrish   **D.** Essex Johnson

7. Cleveland might not have much luck drafting quarterbacks in the first round, but it did hit on this 13th-round selection.

A. Otto Graham   **B.** Bernie Kosar   **C.** Frank Ryan   **D.** Brian Sipe

8. The Ravens rarely needed to look outside the first two rounds to find playmakers, but with the 207th pick in 2002, Baltimore picked this offensive weapon.

A. Ovie Mughelli   **B.** Josh Scobey   **C.** Chester Taylor   **D.** Brandon Stokely

9. Which of these Bengals running backs was not a second-round selection?

A. Corey Dillion   **B.** Rudi Johnson   **C.** Joe Mixon   **D.** Pete Johnson

10. Which of these quarterbacks was not a Ravens sixth-round pick?

A. Tyrod Taylor   **B.** Derek Anderson   **C.** Trace McSorley   **D.** Tyler Huntley

11. This third-round draft pick in 1998 eventually played a major role in the Steelers winning Super Bowl XL.

A. Hines Ward   **B.** Joey Porter   **C.** Willie Parker   **D.** Antwaan Randle El

12. A Cleveland fifth-round pick from the 1950s, this Hall-of-Famer was making an impact on the NFL well into the 21st century.

A. Joe Gibbs   **B.** Sam Huff   **C.** Dick LeBeau   **D.** Bobby Mitchell

CINCINNATI BENGALS FAST FACTS

Across

2. First player to wear number 1 for the Bengals
4. Coach for Bengals' first Super Bowl appearance
8. Only retired number in franchise history
9. Division Bengals joined when AFL merged with the NFL
10. Started both Super Bowl XVI and XXIII along offensive line and not named Munoz
11. Only Bengals player elected to the Pro Football Hall of Fame
12. First player acquired by the Bengals

Down

1. Nickname of the 1981 AFC Championship Game
3. Johnson who holds the Bengals record for most rushing touchdowns in a career
5. Short-lived last name of Chad Johnson with the Bengals
6. Name of Riverfront Stadium for last four seasons ___ Field
7. First coach who didn't also own the team

HISTORY OF THE CINCINNATI BENGALS

1. Which kicker leads the Bengals in scoring with more than 1,100 points?

A. Evan McPherson   **B.** Mike Nugent   **C.** Shayne Graham   **D.** Jim Breech

2. Who holds the Bengals record for career passing yards?

A. Carson Palmer   **B.** Ken Anderson   **C.** Andy Dalton   **D.** Boomer Esiason

3. Which running back ran for 1,454 yards one year, then topped his own team record by four yards the following season?

A. Corey Dillon   **B.** James Brooks   **C.** Rudi Johnson   **D.** Pete Johnson

4. Who has the most 100-yard receiving games in Cincinnati history?

A. A.J. Green   **B.** Chad Johnson   **C.** Carl Pickens   **D.** Isaac Curtis

5. How many touchdowns did Carl Pickens haul in to set the Bengals record in 1995?

A. 17   **B.** 16   **C.** 15   **D.** 14

6. Who is the only Bengals defender to intercept 10 passes in a season?

A. Louis Breeden   **B.** Leon Hall   **C.** Deltha O'Neal   **D.** Ken Riley

7. Which Bengals player tied Eddie Edwards to become the only Bengals defender with five sacks in a game since sacks became an official NFL statistic?

A. Carlos Dunlap   **B.** Antwon Odom   **C.** Gerald Dixon   **D.** Geno Atkins

8. In 1976, the Bengals set a team record by limiting opponents to how many points per game?

A. 16.9 points   **B.** 16.3 points   **C.** 15.8 points   **D.** 15.0 points

9. What is the largest deficit the Bengals have successfully overcome to win?

A. 27 points   **B.** 24 points   **C.** 23 points   **D.** 21 points

10. How many points did the Bengals score on the Houston Oilers two separate times to set the team record for points in a game?

A. 61   **B.** 63   **C.** 65   **D.** 68

CLEVELAND BROWNS 3 & OUT

1. Rushed for at least 5,000 yards with the Browns

A. Greg Pruitt   **B.** Mike Pruitt   **C.** Earnest Byner   **D.** Kevin Mack

2. Appeared in at least 200 games for Cleveland

A. Doug Dieken   **B.** Clay Matthews   **C.** Phil Dawson   **D.** Ozzie Newsome

3. Threw for 400 yards in a game for the Browns

A. Kelly Holcomb   **B.** Baker Mayfield   **C.** Brian Sipe   **D.** Josh McCown

4. Had worn No. 99 for Cleveland in a game

A. Reggie Camp   **B.** Scott Fujita   **C.** Paul Kruger   **D.** Keith Baldwin

5. Threw at least 80 interceptions for Cleveland

A. Bernie Kosar   **B.** Baker Mayfield   **C.** Mike Phipps   **D.** Frank Ryan

6. Has returned a punt for a touchdown since the Browns re-entered the league

A. Josh Cribbs   **B.** Travis Benjamin   **C.** Jabrill Peppers   **D.** Dennis Northcutt

7. Was drafted by Cleveland in 1999 expansion draft

A. Ty Detmer   **B.** Jim Pyne   **C.** Freddie Solomon   **D.** Kevin Devine

8. Current college head coach who was previously an assistant in Cleveland

A. Kirk Ferentz   **B.** Brian Kelly   **C.** Herm Edwards   **D.** David Shaw

9. Won at least 40 games with the Browns

A. Marty Schottenheimer   **B.** Bill Belichick   **C.** Blanton Collier   **D.** Sam Rutigliano

10. Hosted Browns training camp

A. Kent State   **B.** Bowling Green   **C.** Hiram   **D.** Youngstown State

HISTORY OF THE CLEVELAND BROWNS

1. Who holds the Browns record for most career points?

A. Lou Groza   **B.** Don Cockroft   **C.** Jim Brown   **D.** Phil Dawson

2. Who is the only Browns quarterback to throw for 4,000 yards in a season?

A. Bernie Kosar   **B.** Brian Sipe   **C.** Otto Graham   **D.** Baker Mayfield

3. Jim Brown holds six of the top-seven single-season rushing totals in team histor. Who holds the other spot on the list?

A. Mike Pruitt   **B.** Jamal Lewis   **C.** Peyton Hillis   **D.** Nick Chubb

4. Which of these Browns records is not held by Jim Brown?

A. Rushing touchdowns, career   **B.** Points, season   **C.** Rushing yards, career   **D.** Rushing yards, game

5. Who holds the Cleveland team record for receiving yards in a season?

A. Odell Beckham Jr.   **B.** Ozzie Newsome   **C.** Josh Gordon   **D.** Braylon Edwards

6. Who leads the Browns in career interceptions with 45 across two stints with the team?

A. Ken Konz   **B.** Thom Darden   **C.** Bernie Parrish   **D.** Warren Lahr

7. Who is Cleveland's leader in career sacks?

A. Clay Matthews   **B.** Myles Garrett   **C.** Jerry Sherk   **D.** Bill Glass

8. What is the Browns' record for most points in a game since returning to the NFL in 1999?

A. 63 points   **B.** 57 points   **C.** 51 points   **D.** 45 points

9. In which season did Cleveland set its record for wins in an NFL season?

A. 2020   **B.** 1994   **C.** 1986   **D.** 1980

10. How large was the biggest comeback in Browns history?

A. 22 points   **B.** 25 points   **C.** 27 points   **D.** 28 points

BALTIMORE RAVENS JERSEY MATH

We know everyone hates math, but we think we found a way to make it fun. Simply follow the instructions and come out with the correct number or player being hinted at.

1. If you add Ed Reed to Bart Scott, you'd get the jersey number of the only Ravens player to be named NFL Man of the Year.

   _____

2. When you divide Dennis Pitta by Jimmy Smith, you get the number of this longtime Ravens specialist.

   _____

3. Start with Mark Clayton and take away Ray Lewis and you find the unusual jersey number worn by this Hall-of-Famer during his two seasons in Baltimore.

   _____

4. If you multiply the two quarterbacks who started for the Ravens in the Super Bowl, you earn this number, worn by Kyle Juszczyk during his stop in Baltimore.

   _____

5. This Ravens defensive lineman is the result when you multiply Jamal Lewis by Matt Stover.

   _____

6. When you subtract Patrick Queen from Anquan Bolden, you get this Ravens legend who also found his way into Canton.

   _____

7. Don't be blindsided when you add Lamar Jackson to Michael Oher and you get the number worn by this Hall-of-Famer with the Ravens.

   _____

8. Combine Ovie Mughelli and Peter Boulware and you get the most recent addition to the Ravens Ring of Honor.

   _____

9. When you subtract Derrick Mason from Todd Heap, you find this quarterback, who won both of his starts with the Ravens to end his legendary career.

   _____

10. When you divide Terrell Suggs by Marquise Brown, you get the number of this quarterback, who split starting duties in 2000 but didn't start the Super Bowl.

   _____

HISTORY OF THE BALTIMORE RAVENS

1. Who is Baltimore's leading scorer all-time?

A. Lamar Jackson   **B.** Justin Tucker   **C.** Matt Stover   **D.** Jamal Lewis

2. Who holds the Ravens record for most passing yards in a game with 442?

A. Steve McNair   **B.** Lamar Jackson   **C.** Joe Flacco   **D.** Vinny Testaverde

3. How many times did Jamal Lewis rush for at least 100 yards in his historic 2003 season?

A. 14   **B.** 11   **C.** 13   **D.** 12

4. Who is the Ravens' all-time leader in receptions?

A. Ray Rice   **B.** Derrick Mason   **C.** Todd Heap   **D.** Steve Smith

5. Who holds the Ravens record for receiving yards in a game?

A. Qadry Ismail   **B.** Todd Heap   **C.** Derrick Alexander   **D.** Marquise Brown

6. Whose 17 sacks is the standard for Ravens pass rushers as the team record in a single season?

A. Elvis Dumervil   **B.** Peter Boulware   **C.** Ray Lewis   **D.** Terrell Suggs

7. Which of these Baltimore interception records is not held by Ed Reed?

A. Single-season   **B.** Career   **C.** Consecutive Games   **D.** Touchdowns

8. What is the largest comeback in Ravens history?

A. 20 points   **B.** 21 points   **C.** 23 points   **D.** 24 points

9. How many points did the Ravens score on Miami for their largest win in team history?

A. 54   **B.** 56   **C.** 57   **D.** 59

10. How many points did the Ravens allow in their record-setting 2000 season?

A. 199   **B.** 187   **C.** 176   **D.** 165

PITTSBURGH STEELERS ALMA MATERS

Match the player with where he played his final season of college football before jumping to the NFL.

1. Mel Blount

2. Lynn Swann

3. Hines Ward

4. Ben Roethlisberger

5. Joey Porter

6. John Stallworth

7. James Harrison

8. Jack Butler

9. Jerome Bettis

10. Joe Greene

11. Terry Bradshaw

12. Plaxico Burress

13. Donnie Shell

14. Jack Ham

15. Willie Parker

A. South Carolina State

B. Penn State

C. Notre Dame

D. North Carolina

E. Alabama A&M

F. Michigan State

G. North Texas

H. Kent State

I. Louisiana Tech

J. Southern

K. St. Bonaventure

L. Georgia

M. Miami Ohio

N. USC

O. Colorado State

HISTORY OF THE PITTSBURGH STEELERS

1. Who is Pittsburgh's all-time leading scorer?

A. Chris Boswell   **B.** Jeff Reed   **C.** Gary Andersen   **D.** Shaun Suisham

2. Ben Roethlisberger has nine of the 10 best passing games in Steelers history. Who has the other one?

A. Tommy Maddox   **B.** Mason Rudolph   **C.** Kordell Stewart   **D.** Neil O'Donnell

3. Who holds the Steelers record for rushing yards in a season?

A. Franco Harris   **B.** Barry Foster   **C.** Jerome Bettis   **D.** Le'Veon Bell

4. Who is the only Steelers player to score 100 touchdowns in their career?

A. Jerome Bettis   **B.** Hines Ward   **C.** Franco Harris   **D.** Lynn Swann

5. Which receiver holds the record for most receiving yards in a game?

A. Jimmy Orr   **B.** Antonio Brown   **C.** Plaxico Burress   **D.** JuJu Smith-Schuster

6. Who has the most interceptions in Steelers history with 57?

A. Rod Woodson   **B.** Mel Blount   **C.** Jack Butler   **D.** Donnie Shell

7. Whose 4.5 sacks in 1996 is officially the team record, according to the NFL, despite the Steelers claiming the record belongs to Joe Greene?

A. Levon Kirkland   **B.** Kevin Greene   **C.** Jason Gildon   **D.** Chad Brown

8. What is the Pittsburgh record for most points scored in a game?

A. 55   **B.** 57   **C.** 60   **D.** 63

9. How much was the largest deficit the Steelers have overcome to win in franchise history?

A. 21 points   **B.** 23 points   **C.** 24 points   **D.** 27 points

10. Who did the Steelers defeat 45-0 for their largest shutout victory in team history?

A. Indianapolis Colts   **B.** Cleveland Browns   **C.** Kansas City Chiefs   **D.** New York Jets

AFC South Hunt

```
V B F D F S N A X E T J S A S F O
Q B G Z T G N I N N A M P X A I Q
O J E E G R O E G E B O Z M T N F
P H I L L I P S E Y Z A Z U I D P
D T S I L J T S S F G R R O N I L
H X M S C I S R L G V N F V U A E
V H L O F E V P S L K N U X A F T
Y N Y X N R S N W K E Q Q D Q P T
H E I N O R E I O R E N Y Y F A W
E G E L A B U E K S O X U K J O I
Z T P U H F E W N T K L Y R R L C
L R G U W G M B S E D C Y I B I H
T A D W W K U K N M Y Q A A M S R
J S N A T I T O I N U N L J T B L
H A R R I S O N C K C T B R H E D
W J C O L T S M E M R X L E Y F P
P F H O U S T O N W R X D G I J E
```

Brunell	Houston	Phillips
Colts	Indianapolis	Taylor
Coughlin	Jacksonville	Tennessee
Dungy	Jaguars	Texans
Freeney	Leftwich	Titans
George	Manning	Unitas
Harrison	McNair	

KNOW YOUR DRAFT: AFC SOUTH

1. The Colts certainly got a steal in 2003 when they drafted Robert Mathis in which round out of Alabama A&M?

A. 4th   **B.** 5th   **C.** 6th   **D.** 7th

2. Ken Houston was one of the many steals the Titans had in their early days as the Houston Oilers, drafting the defensive back in which round?

A. 8th   **B.** 9th   **C.** 11th   **D.** 12th

3. The Texans drafted this eventual playoff-starting quarterback in the fifth round.

A. T.J. Yates   **B.** Deshaun Watson   **C.** Tom Savage   **D.** Brian Hoyer

4. This 2016 third-round pick has made a comfortable living chasing quarterbacks after being drafted by Jacksonville.

A. Trey Hendrickson   **B.** Danielle Hunter   **C.** Yannick Ngakoue   **D.** Frank Clark

5. The Titans franchise has a history of success at finding pass catchers in the fourth round, but which one of these players was not a fourth-round selection by Tennessee?

A. Charley Taylor   **B.** Charlie Joiner   **C.** Steve Largent   **D.** Derrick Mason

6. In 1954, the Colts found a pair of steals in the draft, longtime starting guard Alex Sandusky in the 16th round, and this future Hall-of-Famer in the 20th.

A. Lenny Moore   **B.** Chuck Noll   **C.** Ron Mix   **D.** Raymond Berry

7. This longtime Jaguars starting quarterback didn't come out of college with a lot of hype, which is how Jacksonville was able to draft him in the fourth round.

A. Gardner Minshew   **B.** Byron Leftwich   **C.** Rob Johnson   **D.** David Garrard

8. This 2009 fourth-round pick ended up having a moderate amount of NFL success and has the most interceptions of any Texans draft pick.

A. Sherrick McManis   **B.** Kareem Jackson   **C.** Glover Quin   **D.** Andre Hal

9. Which of these Jaguars legends was actually drafted originally by Jacksonville?

A. Keenan McCardell   **B.** Fred Taylor   **C.** Mark Brunell   **D.** Jimmy Smith

10. Although he's performed like a first-round pick, in which round did the Titans actually draft Derrick Henry?

A. 3rd   **B.** 7th   **C.** 2nd   **D.** 4th

11. In which round did the Texans nab their all-time leading rusher?

A. 5th   **B.** 6th   **C.** 7th   **D.** Undrafted

12. Who was not a No. 1 overall pick from the Colts franchise?

A. George Shaw   **B.** Marshall Faulk   **C.** Jeff George   **D.** Bubba Smith

INDIANAPOLIS COLTS 3 & OUT

Can you spot the odd-man out? Three of these answers actually answer the prompt, so your job is to spot the outlier.

1. Caught at least 10 passes in a Colts playoff game

A. Pierre Garcon   **B.** Dallas Clark   **C.** Reggie Wayne   **D.** Joseph Addai

2. Played at least 200 games for the Colts

A. Jeff Saturday   **B.** Johnny Unitas   **C.** Peyton Manning   **D.** Adam Vinatieri

3. Led the Colts in scoring in a season

A. Jonathan Taylor   **B.** Joseph Addai   **C.** Edgerrin James   **D.** Marshall Faulk

4. Has at least 200 receiving yards in a game for the Colts

A. Marvin Harrison   **B.** Pierre Garcon   **C.** Reggie Wayne   **D.** Jimmy Orr

5. Recorded at least four sacks in a game for the Colts

A. Chad Bratzke   **B.** Dwight Freeney   **C.** Robert Mathis   **D.** Johnie Cooks

6. Returned multiple kickoffs for a touchdown with the Colts

A. Terrence Wilkins   **B.** Aaron Bailey   **C.** Dominic Rhodes   **D.** Jim Duncan

7. Made five field goals in a game for Indianapolis

A. Cary Blanchard   **B.** Mike Vanderjagt   **C.** Toni Linhart   **D.** Dean Biasucci

8. Former NFL head coach that spent time as assistant with the Colts

A. Chuck Noll   **B.** Leslie Frazier   **C.** Vic Fangio   **D.** Bill Callahan

9. Named Associated Press Coach of the Year with the Colts

A. Tony Dungy   **B.** Ted Marchibroda   **C.** Weeb Ewbank   **D.** Bruce Arians

10. Awarded NFL MVP by the Associated Press as a member of the Colts

A. Bert Jones   **B.** Earl Morrall   **C.** Marshall Faulk   **D.** Johnny Unitas

HISTORY OF THE INDIANAPOLIS COLTS

1. Who is Indianapolis' all-time leading scorer?

A. Dean Biasucci   **B.** Adam Vinatieri   **C.** Mike Vanderjagt   **D.** Marvin Harrison

2. Who holds the Colts' record for passing yards in a season?

A. Peyton Manning   **B.** Philip Rivers   **C.** Johnny Unitas   **D.** Andrew Luck

3. Who has scored the most rushing touchdowns in Colts history?

A. Edgerrin James   **B.** Lenny Moore   **C.** Joseph Addai   **D.** Tom Matte

4. Which running back holds the record for most rushing yards in a game?

A. Edgerrin James   **B.** Marshall Faulk   **C.** Eric Dickerson   **D.** Jonathan Taylor

5. Which receiver holds the record for most games with at least one catch?

A. Marvin Harrison   **B.** Raymond Berry   **C.** Reggie Wayne   **D.** T.Y. Hilton

6. Who has the most receiving yards in Colts history?

A. Raymond Berry   **B.** Marvin Harrison   **C.** T.Y. Hilton   **D.** Reggie Wayne

7. Who has the most sacks in Colts history?

A. Johnie Cooks   **B.** Dwight Freeney   **C.** Robert Mathis   **D.** Chad Bratzke

8. In which season did the Colts set their team record for most points in a season?

A. 2004   **B.** 2005   **C.** 2007   **D.** 2009

9. Who did the Colts defeat 56-0 for the largest win in team history?

A. Green Bay Packers   **B.** Detroit Lions   **C.** Chicago Bears   **D.** New York Giants

10. In the 2013 playoffs, how large was the deficit from which the Colts rallied to knock off the Chiefs?

A. 24 points   **B.** 25 points   **C.** 27 points   **D.** 28 points

JACKSONVILLE JAGUARS JERSEY MATH

We know everyone hates math, but we think we found a way to make it fun. Simply follow the instructions and come out with the correct number or player being hinted at.

1. The difference between the two numbers James Robinson wore in the 2020 season is this controversial quarterback who started 73 games for Jacksonville and led the Jaguars to the AFC title game.

    _____

2. When you add together Tony Brackens and David Garrard, you get this half of Jacksonville's dominant defensive line duo.

    _____

3. Combining Mark Brunell and Byron Leftwich results in this wide receiver who was one of the many stars who bargained their way out of Jacksonville.

    _____

4. If you instead multiplied Mark Brunell and Byron Lefwich, it would come out to this linebacker who played for the Jaguars toward the end of his career.

    _____

5. Add Trevor Lawrence to Tony Boselli and you get this Jaguars receiver who played a key role in the Jaguars' early success.

    _____

6. If you combined the two greatest running backs in Jaguars history, Fred Taylor and Maurice Jones-Drew, you'd get this number, most recently worn by A.J. Cann.

    _____

7. Subtract Josh Scobee from Paul Posluszny to find this ferocious pass rusher who is anchoring the Jaguars defense.

    _____

8. What happens when you add together Jalen Ramsey and Leonard Fournette? You get this number that made its debut in Jacksonville in 2016 on Jarrod Wilson.

    _____

9. Renaldo Wynn and Mike Hollis were mashed together, resulting in this dominant defensive tackle at the heart of the early Jaguars defenses.

    _____

10. If you added up every quarterback who started for the Jaguars in the 1990s, you'd still be a touchdown and extra point short of this franchise legend who was a quarterback's best friend.

    _____

HISTORY OF THE JACKSONVILLE JAGUARS

1. Who has scored the most points in Jaguars history?

A. Maurice Jones-Drew   **B.** Mike Hollis   **C.** Josh Scobee   **D.** Fred Taylor

2. Which quarterback has completed the most passes in a season in Jaguars history?

A. Trevor Lawrence   **B.** Gardner Minshew   **C.** Blake Bortles   **D.** David Garrard

3. Who holds the Jaguars record for most career rushing touchdowns?

A. James Stewart   **B.** Maurice Jones-Drew   **C.** Leonard Fournette   **D.** Fred Taylor

4. Which Jaguars receiver holds the team record with 291 receiving yards in a game?

A. Jimmy Smith   **B.** Allen Robinson   **C.** Keenan McCardell   **D.** Justin Blackmon

5. In which year did Jimmy Smith lead the NFL with a team-record 116 receptions?

A. 2002   **B.** 2001   **C.** 2000   **D.** 1999

6. Who has the most interceptions in Jacksonville history with 30?

A. Marlon McCree   **B.** Jalen Ramsey   **C.** Aaron Beasley   **D.** Rashean Mathis

7. Who sacked the quarterback 14.5 times to set the Jaguars single-season sacks record?

A. Kevin Hardy   **B.** Calais Campbell   **C.** Yannick Ngakoue   **D.** Tony Brackens

8. What is Jacksonville's record for most points scored in a game?

A. 48   **B.** 49   **C.** 51   **D.** 54

9. What was the final margin of victory in 2000 when the Jaguars defeated Cleveland for the biggest win in team history?

A. 48 points   **B.** 44 points   **C.** 42 points   **D.** 39 points

10. The only time the Jaguars have ever rallied from 20 points or more down to win came in 2014 when they defeated which team?

A. Indianapolis Colts   **B.** Houston Texans   **C.** New York Giants   **D.** Detroit Lions

HOUSTON TEXANS FAST FACTS

Across

3. Coach who led Houston to the playoffs for the first time

7. First head coach in franchise history

8. Man responsible for bringing football back to Houston

11. First pick in 2002 expansion draft

12. Receiver who wrote the Texans record book

Down

1. Only coach with a winning record in Houston

2. Quarterback who started first playoff game in franchise history

4. First quarterback to throw for 4,000 yards in a season

5. First first-team All-Pro player

6. First draft pick made by Houston in the entry draft

9. The most recent Texans player to be named Defensive Rookie of the Year

10. Last player taken No. 1 overall by the Texans

HISTORY OF THE HOUSTON TEXANS

1. Who is Houston's all-time leading scorer?

A. Kris Brown   **B.** Andre Johnson   **C.** Ka'imi Fairbairn   **D.** Randy Bullock

2. Who holds the Texans record with six touchdown passes in a game?

A. David Carr   **B.** Ryan Fitzpatrick   **C.** Matt Schaub   **D.** Deshaun Watson

3. How many rushing touchdowns did Arian Foster score in 2010 to set the Texans' single-season record?

A. 17   **B.** 16   **C.** 15   **D.** 14

4. Who has caught the most touchdown passes in team history?

A. Owen Daniels   **B.** DeAndre Hopkins   **C.** Will Fuller V   **D.** Andre Johnson

5. Who has scored the most total touchdowns in Houston's history?

A. Dominick Williams   **B.** DeAndre Hopkins   **C.** Arian Foster   **D.** Andre Johnson

6. How many sacks did J.J. Watt have in his Texans career to set the franchise record?

A. 96   **B.** 98.5   **C.** 101.0   **D.** 103.5

7. Whose seven interceptions still stand as the Texans' single-season record?

A. Marcus Coleman   **B.** Jonathan Joseph   **C.** Kareem Jackson   **D.** Dunta Robinson

8. In which year did the Texans set their team record with 12 wins?

A. 2012   **B.** 2016   **C.** 2018   **D.** 2019

9. How many points did the Texans score on Tennessee to set their franchise record for points in a game?

A. 51   **B.** 54   **C.** 57   **D.** 60

10. Houston's largest comeback win came in 2013 when it rallied from 21 points to defeat which team?

A. Miami Dolphins   **B.** San Diego Chargers   **C.** Kansas City Chiefs   **D.** New York Jets

TENNESSEE TITANS ALMA MATERS

Match the player with where he played his final season of college football before jumping to the NFL.

1. Bruce Matthews		A. Idaho	
2. Earl Campbell		B. Syracuse	
3. Warren Moon		C. Alabama	
4. Frank Wycheck		D. North Carolina A&T	
5. Eddie George		E. Washington	
6. Mike Munchak		F. USC	
7. Keith Bulluck		G. Utah	
8. Steve McNair		H. Texas A&M	
9. Ray Childress		I. Texas	
10. Chris Johnson		J. Ohio State	
11. Elvin Bethea		K. Maryland	
12. Jim Norton		L. Alcorn State	
13. Kevin Dyson		M. Florida	
14. Derrick Henry		N. Penn State	
15. Jevon Kearse		O. East Carolina	

HISTORY OF THE TENNESSEE TITANS

1. Who is the Titans' all-time leading scorer?

A. Ryan Succop   **B.** Rob Bironas   **C.** Al Del Greco   **D.** George Blanda

2. Who is the only Titans quarterback to throw for 500 yards in a game?

A. Warren Moon   **B.** Billy Volek   **C.** Steve McNair   **D.** Marcus Mariota

3. Who holds the Titans record for rushing yards in a game?

A. Earl Campbell   **B.** Derrick Henry   **C.** Eddie George   **D.** Chris Johnson

4. Who holds the Tennessee record for career receiving yards?

A. Drew Hill   **B.** Ernest Givens   **C.** Frank Wycheck   **D.** Charlie Hennigan

5. Who has scored the most touchdowns in team history with 74 trips to the end zone?

A. Chris Johnson   **B.** Derrick Henry   **C.** Earl Campbell   **D.** Eddie George

6. Who has the most interceptions in Titans history with 45 picks?

A. Jim Norton   **B.** Freddy Glick   **C.** Kevin Byard   **D.** Ken Houston

7. Who do the Titans credit as their single-season sack leader with 17 in a year?

A. Ray Childress   **B.** Elvin Bethea   **C.** Jesse Baker   **D.** William Fuller

8. What is the most points the Titans have scored in a game since moving to Tennessee?

A. 57   **B.** 54   **C.** 51   **D.** 48

9. Everyone knows about that one comeback on this franchise, but what is Tennessee's largest comeback victory?

A. 21 points   **B.** 23 points   **C.** 24 points   **D.** 27 points

10. Who did the then-Oilers clobber 55-0 for their largest victory in team history?

A. New York Jets   **B.** Buffalo Bills   **C.** Kansas City Chiefs   **D.** Oakland Raiders

AFC West Hunt

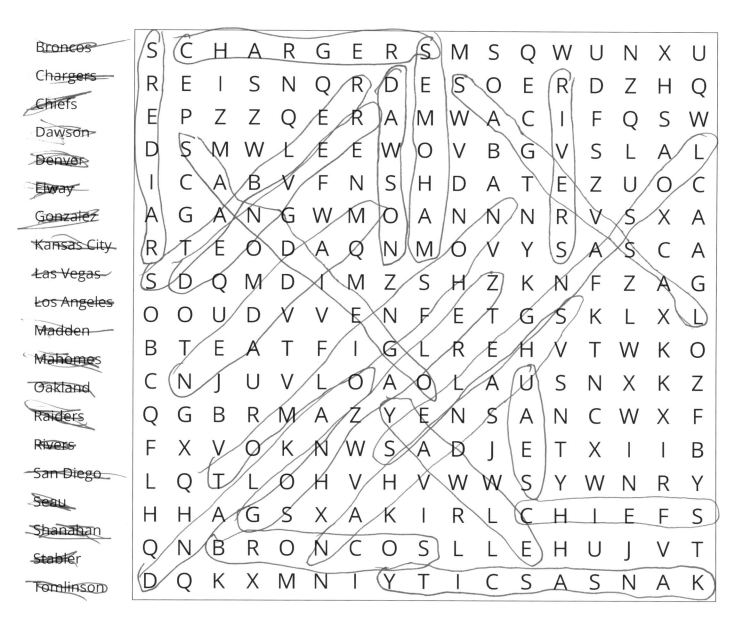

KNOW YOUR DRAFT: AFC WEST

1. The fourth round of the Broncos' 2006 draft was extremely successful, but who was not one of their three picks in that round?

A. Brandon Marshall   **B.** Dominique Foxworth   **C.** Elvis Dumervil   **D.** Domenik Hixon

2. In which round did the Chiefs draft their all-time leading rusher, Jamaal Charles?

A. 3rd   **B.** 4th   **C.** 5th   **D.** 6th

3. Which of the current AFC West members actually drafted Lance Alworth in the 1962 AFL Draft?

A. Chiefs   **B.** Broncos   **C.** Raiders   **D.** Chargers

4. One of several Hall of Famers drafted in the AFL but never played in the league, who did the Chargers draft in 1961?

A. Bob Lily   **B.** Herb Adderley   **C.** Jimmy Johnson   **D.** Merlin Olsen

5. In which year did the Raiders use their second-round selection on Howie Long?

A. 1979   **B.** 1980   **C.** 1982   **D.** 1981

6. In which round was Kansas City able to draft Joe Horn, Tyreek Hill and Dante Hall?

A. 7th   **B.** 6th   **C.** 5th   **D.** 4th

7. The Broncos picked this future Hall of Famer in the AFL Draft even though he didn't end up playing in Denver.

A. Dick Butkus   **B.** Gale Sayers   **C.** Roger Staubach   **D.** Mike Ditka

8. In which round of the 2013 draft did the Chargers pick up Keenan Allen?

A. 3rd   **B.** 4th   **C.** 5th   **D.** 6th

9. The Chargers 2004 draft is known more for the Eli Manning trade, but which of these other players was selected that year?

A. Darren Sproles   **B.** Nick Hardwick   **C.** Marcus McNeill   **D.** Vincent Jackson

10. In which year did the Broncos use a sixth-round pick to draft Terrell Davis?

A. 1992   **B.** 1993   **C.** 1994   **D.** 1995

11. Which of these famous Raiders quarterbacks was actually drafted by the franchise?

A. Rich Gannon   **B.** Cotton Davidson   **C.** Jim Plunkett   **D.** Ken Stabler

12. Which of these pass rushers was not actually drafted by the Chiefs?

A. Scott Fujita   **B.** Curley Culp   **C.** Jared Allen   **D.** Justin Houston

DENVER BRONCOS 3 & OUT

Can you spot the odd-man out? Three of these answers actually answer the prompt, so your job is to spot the outlier.

1. Voted NFL MVP by the Associated Press while with the Broncos

A. Clinton Portis   **B.** Terrell Davis   **C.** Peyton Manning   **D.** John Elway

2. Named Defensive Player of the Year or Defensive Rookie of the Year by the Associated Press with Denver

A. Randy Gradishar   **B.** Bradly Chubb   **C.** Mike Croel   **D.** Von Miller

3. Ran for 200 yards in a game with the Broncos

A. Knowshon Moreno   **B.** Mike Anderson   **C.** Sammy Winder   **D.** Terrell Davis

4. Threw for 10,000 yards in his Broncos career

A. Craig Morton   **B.** Jake Plummer   **C.** Brian Griese   **D.** Jay Cutler

5. Intercepted at least four passes in a game for Denver

A. Goose Gonsulin   **B.** Champ Bailey   **C.** Deltha O'Neal   **D.** Willie Brown

6. Did not return two kickoffs for a touchdown in the same season for Denver

A. Goldie Sellers   **B.** Trindon Holliday   **C.** Deltha O'Neal   **D.** Eddie Royal

7. Did not win at least 60 percent of total games coached with Denver

A. Red Miller   **B.** Wade Phillips   **C.** Dan Reeves   **D.** John Ralston

8. Number is retired by Denver

A. Floyd Little   **B.** John Elway   **C.** Randy Gradishar   **D.** Frank Tripucka

9. Named to at least five Pro Bowls with the Broncos

A. Shannon Sharpe   **B.** Rod Smith   **C.** Demaryius Thomas   **D.** Tom Nalen

10. A principal or majority owner in the Broncos

A. Edgar Kaiser   **B.** Gerald Phipps   **C.** Robert Howsam   **D.** Calvin Kunz

HISTORY OF THE DENVER BRONCOS

1. Who is the Broncos' all-time leading scorer?

A. Jason Elam   **B.** Terrell Davis   **C.** Matt Prater   **D.** Jim Turner

2. Who holds the Broncos record for most passing touchdowns in a game?

A. Jake Plummer   **B.** Craig Morton   **C.** Peyton Manning   **D.** John Elway

3. Who holds the Broncos record for rushing yards in a game?

A. Terrell Davis   **B.** Mike Anderson   **C.** Clinton Portis   **D.** Knowshon Moreno

4. Who holds the Denver record for most receptions in a single season?

A. Demaryius Thomas   **B.** Ed McCaffrey   **C.** Rod Smith   **D.** Brandon Marshall

5. Who set the Broncos record for receiving yards in a season with 1,619?

A. Rod Smith   **B.** Emmanuel Sanders   **C.** Brandon Marshall   **D.** Demaryius Thomas

6. In which year did Von Miller set Denver's single-season sack record with 18.5?

A. 2012   **B.** 2014   **C.** 2016   **D.** 2018

7. Who holds the Broncos record for career interceptions with 44?

A. Tyrone Braxton   **B.** Goose Gonsoulin   **C.** Champ Bailey   **D.** Steve Foley

8. What is the Denver record for the most points it has scored in a single-game?

A. 50   **B.** 52   **C.** 54   **D.** 56

9. Who did the Broncos beat for their only win of at least 40 points?

A. Oakland Raiders   **B.** New York Jets   **C.** San Diego Chargers   **D.** Chicago Bears

10. The Broncos have rallied from which deficit three times to set then tie the franchise record for largest comeback victory?

A. 20 points   **B.** 21 points   **C.** 24 points   **D.** 25 points

LOS ANGELES CHARGERS JERSEY MATH

We know everyone hates math, but we think we found a way to make it fun. Simply follow the instructions and come out with the correct number or player being hinted at.

1. Mike Scifres multiplied by Ryan Leaf results in this Hall-of-Fame tight end whose son also played in the league.

_____

2. Natrone Means combines with Dick Harris to create this lights-out linebacker for the Chargers.

_____

3. Adding Dan Fouts to Lorenzo Neal results in this Hall-of-Fame linebacker whose first name doesn't match the impact he had on the field.

_____

4. Austin Ekeler divided by Justin Herbert is this legendary Chargers kicker who would be very much out of place at the circus.

_____

5. Nate Kaeding added to Nick Hardwick results in this Hall-of-Fame defensive end who began his career with the Chargers.

_____

6. When you multiply Keenan Allen and Rolf Benirschke together, you get this legendary Chargers offensive lineman who paved the way in the franchise's early years.

_____

7. Leslie O'Neal zoomed past and subtracted Ron Mix en route to the resulting quarterback who led the Chargers for a record 225 consecutive games.

_____

8. Lance Alworth joined forces with Charlie Joiner to create this number made popular by Rodney Harrison.

_____

9. Taking away LaDanian Tomlinson from Antonio Gates would be a tough break for the Chargers offense, even if it results in this number worn by Pat Shea in the inaugural 1962 season.

_____

10. Adding together Darren Sproles and Leslie Duncan leaves you a simple extra point shy of this receiver who still holds the franchise record for receiving yards in a game.

_____

HISTORY OF THE LOS ANGELES CHARGERS

1. Who holds the Chargers' career scoring record?

A. Rolf Benirschke   **B.** LaDainian Tomlinson   **C.** Nate Kaeding   **D.** John Carney

2. Who holds the Chargers single-season record for passing yards?

A. Philip Rivers   **B.** John Hadl   **C.** Dan Fouts   **D.** Drew Brees

3. How many touchdowns did LaDainian Tomlinson score in his record-breaking 2006 season?

A. 26   **B.** 27   **C.** 28   **D.** 29

4. LaDainian Tomlinson's production from 2002-2007 occupies six of the top-seven spots in the Chargers record book. Who ranks sixth in single-season rushing yards to break up the Tomlinson party?

A. Natrone Means   **B.** Melvin Gordon   **C.** Ryan Mathews   **D.** Marion Butts

5. Who holds the Chargers (and NFL) record for most receiving touchdowns in a game?

A. Antonio Gates   **B.** Kellen Winslow   **C.** Wes Chandler   **D.** Lance Alworth

6. Who tops the Chargers record book with 42 career interceptions?

A. Rodney Harrison   **B.** Gill Byrd   **C.** Antonio Cromartie   **D.** Charlie McNeil

7. Who holds the Chargers record for both career and single-game sack totals?

A. Leslie O'Neal   **B.** Shawn Merriman   **C.** Gary Johnson   **D.** Shaun Phillips

8. In which season did the Chargers set their franchise record for victories?

A. 2012   **B.** 2009   **C.** 2008   **D.** 2006

9. How many points did the Chargers score in 1963 against Denver to set the franchise record for scoring?

A. 51   **B.** 54   **C.** 56   **D.** 58

10. Which of these opponents were not the victim of a record-tying 21-point comeback win for the Chargers?

A. Arizona Cardinals   **B.** San Francisco 49ers   **C.** Seattle Seahawks   **D.** Cincinnati Bengals

KANSAS CITY CHIEFS FAST FACTS

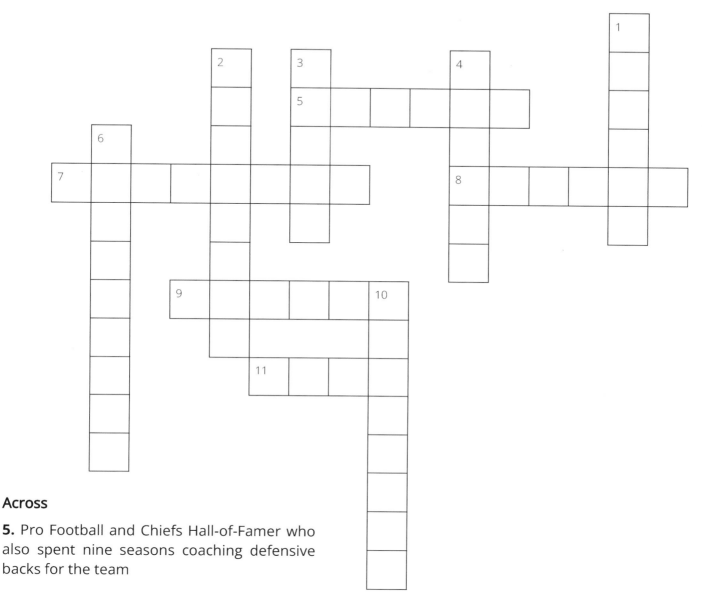

Across

5. Pro Football and Chiefs Hall-of-Famer who also spent nine seasons coaching defensive backs for the team

7. Hall-of-Fame defensive lineman with number 86 retired in his honor

8. Only player named to NFL's 75th anniversary team who played more than two seasons in Kansas City

9. City where franchise was originally formed as part of AFL

11. Number of Chiefs to be named Walter Payton Man of the Year

Down

1. First Chiefs player to be AP Offensive Player of the Year

2. Lamar Hunt's right-hand man and only other non-player or coach honored in Chiefs Hall of Fame

3. First coach in franchise history

4. Non-tight end with most receiving yards in franchise history

6. Where the Chiefs played before Arrowhead: ____ Stadium

10. First kicker inducted into the Pro Football Hall of Fame

HISTORY OF THE KANSAS CITY CHIEFS

1. Who is the Chiefs' all-time leading scorer?

A. Ryan Succop   **B.** Jan Stenerud   **C.** Harrison Butker   **D.** Nick Lowery

2. Which Chiefs quarterback holds the record for most passes completed in a game?

A. Joe Montana   **B.** Elvis Grbac   **C.** Patrick Mahomes   **D.** Alex Smith

3. Who holds the Kansas City record for career rushing yards?

A. Jamaal Charles   **B.** Larry Johnson   **C.** Christian Okoye   **D.** Priest Holmes

4. Who holds the Chiefs record for receiving yards by a non-tight end?

A. Stephone Paige   **B.** Otis Taylor   **C.** Tyreek Hill   **D.** Dwayne Bowe

5. Who gained 309 receiving yards in a game to set the Chiefs record?

A. Carlos Carson   **B.** Tyreek Hill   **C.** Tony Gonzalez   **D.** Stephone Paige

6. Who holds the Kansas City record for most career interceptions?

A. Emmitt Thomas   **B.** Deron Cherry   **C.** Johnny Robinson   **D.** Albert Lewis

7. Who holds the Chiefs single-season record for sacks?

A. Derrick Thomas   **B.** Jared Allen   **C.** Justin Houston   **D.** Tamba Hali

8. What is the Chiefs record for most points scored in a game?

A. 54   **B.** 56   **C.** 59   **D.** 62

9. Who was on the losing end of Kansas City's biggest shutout victory, a 49-0 triumph in 2002?

A. Arizona Cardinals   **B.** Denver Broncos   **C.** New York Jets   **D.** Jacksonville Jaguars

10. What is the largest fourth-quarter deficit Kansas City has overcome to win?

A. 14 points   **B.** 17 points   **C.** 20 points   **D.** 21 points

LAS VEGAS RAIDERS ALMA MATERS

Match the player with where he played his final season of college football before jumping to the NFL.

1. Tim Brown		**A.** USC
2. Howie Long		**B.** Miami
3. Jim Otto		**C.** Maryland Eastern Shore
4. Willie Brown		**D.** Alabama
5. Gene Upshaw		**E.** Pacific
6. Ken Stabler		**F.** Florida State
7. Fred Biletnikoff		**G.** Villanova
8. Art Shell		**H.** Fresno State
9. Marcus Allen		**I.** Notre Dame
10. Tom Flores		**J.** Texas A&M-Kingsville
11. Ray Guy		**K.** Southern Mississippi
12. Rich Gannon		**L.** Grambling
13. Greg Townsend		**M.** TCU
14. Jack Tatum		**N.** Delaware
15. Derek Carr		**O.** Ohio State

HISTORY OF THE LAS VEGAS RAIDERS

1. Who is the Raiders' all-time leading scorer?

A. Tim Brown   **B.** Sebastian Janikowski   **C.** Chris Bahr   **D.** George Blanda

2. Who holds the Raiders record for most career passing yards?

A. Derek Carr   **B.** Rich Gannon   **C.** Ken Stabler   **D.** Jim Plunkett

3. Who is the only Raiders running back to rush for 1,300 yards in a season?

A. Mark van Eeghen   **B.** Darren McFadden   **C.** Marcus Allen   **D.** Napoleon Kaufman

4. Who now holds the Raiders record for catches in a season?

A. Amari Cooper   **B.** Hunter Renfrow   **C.** Tim Brown   **D.** Darren Waller

5. Who holds the Raiders record for receiving yards in a game?

A. Warren Wells   **B.** Amari Cooper   **C.** Tim Brown   **D.** Art Powell

6. Who set the Raiders record for sacks in a season to become the only Raiders player to lead the NFL in sacks?

A. Bill Pickel   **B.** Derrick Burgess   **C.** Khalil Mack   **D.** Howie Long

7. Which defensive back recorded a third of his Raiders-record 39 career interceptions to set the franchise record for single-season interceptions?

A. Eddie Macon   **B.** Willie Brown   **C.** Charles Woodson   **D.** Lester Hayes

8. In which season did the Raiders set their franchise record for points in a season?

A. 1967   **B.** 1983   **C.** 2000   **D.** 2002

9. How many points did the Raiders score in 2010 against Denver to set the franchise single-game scoring record?

A. 52   **B.** 56   **C.** 59   **D.** 63

10. What is the largest comeback victory for the Raiders franchise?

A. 27 points   **B.** 24 points   **C.** 23 points   **D.** 21 points

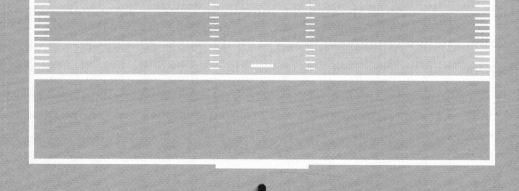

CHAPTER

3

THIRD DOWN
National Football Conference

NFC East Hunt

```
E Y Q I M A H G N I N N U C C K D
U M R N O T G N I H S A W Z H R P
A N B A R B E R V K J H O R Y K F
F U A C O M M A N D E R S P X Y T
M F W H S T N A I G K N I D V X A
K M Z T A W O T P J Y E A L M I Y
R O C R I R R P P S N L I V W G L
Y N E N P C R S F A Y X R C V K R
W A K U L C V G S N A M K I A I U
E B H V E E I G I C V Z Q E A S N
N B L L D S A V N B O W G O I T N
I G L Q A G A G Y I B W J J Q Z T
Z S J L L O D T L J N S B J S O F
M J U Y I H M G O E Q N J O J Z P
F A R U H V V G Z D S R A Q Y H B
G E J L P L Z E E C J T W M D S B
```

KNOW YOUR DRAFT: NFC EAST

1. Which member of the 1972 Dolphins perfect team was actually drafted by the Eagles?

A. Mercury Morris   **B.** Earl Morrall   **C.** Bill Stanfill   **D.** Bob Kuechenberg

2. The Giants used their first-round pick in the 1984 USFL Supplemental Draft on this Hall-of-Famer.

A. Gary Zimmerman   **B.** Jimbo Covert   **C.** Harry Carson   **D.** Kevin Greene

3. Tony Romo went undrafted, but this other Cowboys quarterback was a 10th-round selection for Dallas.

A. Don Meredith   **B.** Roger Staubach   **C.** John Hadl   **D.** Danny White

4. Which of these tight ends was not originally a Washington draft pick?

A. Christian Fauria   **B.** Frank Wycheck   **C.** Robert Royal   **D.** Chris Cooley

5. In which round were the Cowboys able to draft Herschel Walker in 1985?

A. 3rd   **B.** 4th   **C.** 5th   **D.** 6th

6. The Giants have had a lot of success finding players in the second round, but which of these difference makers was not a second-round pick?

A. Michael Strahan   **B.** Tiki Barber   **C.** Amani Toomer   **D.** Brandon Jacobs

7. Which of these ball carriers was not a third-round pick by the Eagles?

A. LeSean McCoy   **B.** Brian Westbrook   **C.** Duce Staley   **D.** Wray Carlton

8. In which round did Washington draft Dexter Manley in the 1981 draft?

A. 9th   **B.** 7th   **C.** 6th   **D.** 5th

9. Only three running backs drafted by Washington have rushed for 5,000 yards in the NFL. Which was the highest drafted of the bunch?

A. Larry Brown   **B.** Alfred Morris   **C.** Stephen Davis   **D.** Brian Mitchell

10. In which round were the Eagles able to pick Trent Cole during the 2005 draft?

A. 4th   **B.** 5th   **C.** 6th   **D.** 7thState

11. Which ball-hawking defensive back did the Giants draft in the 13th round in 1965?

A. Willie Williams   **B.** Henry Carr   **C.** Spider Lockhart   **D.** Clarence Childs

12. In which year did the Cowboys use a third-round selection to draft Jason Witten?

A. 2002   **B.** 2003   **C.** 2004   **D.** 2005

WASHINGTON COMMANDERS ALMA MATERS

Match the player with where he played his final season of college football before jumping to the NFL.

1. Darrell Green	**A.** Pittsburgh
2. Art Monk	**B.** Kansas
3. Len Hauss	**C.** Arizona State
4. Chris Cooley	**D.** Syracuse
5. Charley Taylor	**E.** TCU
6. Joe Theismann	**F.** Louisville
7. Russ Grimm	**G.** Miami
8. John Riggins	**H.** Utah State
9. Sonny Jurgenson	**I.** Central Arkansas
10. Joe Jacoby	**J.** Georgia
11. Larry Brown	**K.** Purdue
12. Ryan Kerrigan	**L.** Duke
13. Clinton Portis	**M.** Kansas State
14. Sammy Baugh	**N.** Texas A&M-Kingsville
15. Monte Coleman	**O.** Notre Dame

HISTORY OF THE WASHINGTON COMMANDERS

1. Who is Washington's all-time leading scorer?

A. Mark Moseley ⭕   **B.** John Riggins   **C.** Chip Lohmiller   **D.** Dustin Hopkins

2. Who holds Washington's single-game record for passing yards?

A. Mark Rypien   **B.** Jason Campbell   **C.** Brad Johnson ⭕   **D.** Kirk Cousins

3. Who holds the franchise record for career rushing yards?

A. Larry Brown   **B.** John Riggins ⭕   **C.** Clinton Portis   **D.** Stephen Davis

4. Who set the Washington single-season rushing yards record in the 21st century?

A. Antonio Gibson   **B.** Alfred Morris ⭕   **C.** Ladell Betts   **D.** Clinton Portis

5. Who holds the Commanders record for receiving yards in a season?

A. Charley Taylor   **B.** Art Monk   **C.** Bobby Mitchell   **D.** Santana Moss ⭕

6. How many interceptions did Darrell Green have during his career in Washington?

A. 46   **B.** 49   **C.** 51   **D.** 54 ⭕

7. Whose 97.5 career sacks is the Commanders' record?

A. Dexter Manley ⭕   **B.** Brian Orakpo   **C.** Ryan Kerrigan   **D.** Charles Mann

8. How many points did Washington score in a 1966 game to set the NFL single-game scoring record?

A. 70   **B.** 71   **C.** 72 ⭕   **D.** 73

9. How badly did Washington defeat Detroit on opening day 1991 to set the franchise record for largest margin of victory?

A. 41 points   **B.** 42 points   **C.** 45 points ⭕   **D.** 47 points

10. Who was the victim of Washington's biggest comeback victory, a 24-point rally in 2015?

A. San Francisco 49ers   **B.** Tampa Bay Buccaneers ⭕   **C.** Atlanta Falcons   **D.** New York Giants

DALLAS COWBOYS FAST FACTS

Across

4. Original owner of the Cowboys

6. General manager who helped negotiate AFL-NFL merger

10. Stadium where Cowboys played before Texas Stadium

11. The Hall-of-Famer who comes first alphabetically among those who played at least two seasons for the Cowboys

12. The only player to win Super Bowl MVP on the losing team

Down

1. The only NFC team with a winning record against Dallas when postseason is factored in

2. First head coach in Cowboys history

3. Running back who holds franchise record for most rushing yards in a season

5. Only person to hold a title within organization in addition to being head coach

7. California city where Cowboys have conducted training camp 15 times since 2001

8. Nickname of first player Cowboys selected with No. 1 overall pick

9. The city where AT&T Stadium is located

HISTORY OF THE DALLAS COWBOYS

1. Who is the Cowboys' all-time leading scorer?

A. Rafael Septien   **B.** Dan Bailey   **C.** Mike Clark   **D.** Emmitt Smith

2. Who holds the Dallas record for most passing yards in a season?

A. Troy Aikman   **B.** Roger Staubach   **C.** Dak Prescott   **D.** Tony Romo

3. Which of these Cowboys rushing records does not belong to Emmitt Smith?

A. Yards, career   **B.** Attempts, game   **C.** Yards, season   **D.** Touchdowns, season

4. Who holds the Cowboys record for single-season receptions?

A. Michael Irvin   **B.** Dez Bryant   **C.** Jason Witten   **D.** Drew Pearson

5. Who holds the Dallas high mark for receiving yards in a game?

A. Bob Hayes   **B.** Miles Austin   **C.** Dez Bryant   **D.** Tony Hill

6. Whose single-season record did Trevon Diggs tie in 2021 with his 11 interceptions?

A. Terrance Newman   **B.** Everson Walls   **C.** Charlie Waters   **D.** Mel Renfro

7. Who is Dallas' all-time leader in sacks?

A. Randy White   **B.** Harvey Martin   **C.** DeMarcus Ware   **D.** Micah Parsons

8. What is the Cowboys record for most team points in a game?

A. 59   **B.** 61   **C.** 64   **D.** 66

9. The Cowboys set their record for largest victory in 1966 when they defeated the Eagles by how many points?

A. 49   **B.** 47   **C.** 44   **D.** 41

10. What is the largest comeback victory for the Cowboys?

A. 27 points   **B.** 24 points   **C.** 23 points   **D.** 21 points

PHILADELPHIA EAGLES 3 & OUT

Can you spot the odd-man out? Three of these answers actually answer the prompt, so your job is to spot the outlier.

1. Number is retired by the Eagles

A. Donovan McNabb   **B.** Brian Dawkins   **C.** Troy Vincent   **D.** Steve Van Buren

2. Named Coach of the Year by the Associated Press with the Eagles

A. Dick Vermeil   **B.** Buck Shaw   **C.** Andy Reid   **D.** Ray Rhodes

3. Played at least 12 seasons for Philadelphia

A. David Akers   **B.** Jason Kelce   **C.** Jason Peters   **D.** Donovan McNabb

4. Threw for 400 yards in a game for the Eagles

A. Randall Cunningham   **B.** Vince Young   **C.** Michael Vick   **D.** Ron Jaworski

5. Ran for 200 yards in a game for Philadelphia

A. LeSean McCoy   **B.** Brian Westbrook   **C.** Duce Staley   **D.** Steve Van Buren

6. Had at least four sacks in a game for the Eagles

A. Clyde Simmons   **B.** Reggie White   **C.** Trent Cole   **D.** Hugh Douglas

7. Has not returned multiple kickoffs and multiple punts for a touchdown

A. DeSean Jackson   **B.** Brian Westbrook   **C.** Derrick Witherspoon   **D.** Brian Mitchell

8. Had a winning record as Philadelphia head coach

A. Ray Rhodes   **B.** Chip Kelly   **C.** Doug Pederson   **D.** Rich Kotite

9. Named to at least five Pro Bowls with the Eagles

A. Jeremiah Trotter   **B.** Fletcher Cox   **C.** Troy Vincent   **D.** Jason Peters

10. One of the Eagles' home fields

A. Franklin Field   **B.** Baker Bowl   **C.** Eagles Stadium   **D.** Connie Mack Stadium

HISTORY OF THE PHILADELPHIA EAGLES

1. Who holds the distinction of being the Eagles' all-time leading scorer?

  A. Jake Elliott   **B.** David Akers   **C.** Sam Baker   **D.** Bobby Walston

2. Who is the only quarterback to throw for 4,000 yards in a season in Eagles history?

  A. Carson Wentz   **B.** Nick Foles   **C.** Donovan McNabb   **D.** Randall Cunningham

3. Who has scored the most rushing touchdowns in Eagles history?

  A. Brian Westbrook   **B.** LeSean McCoy   **C.** Steve Van Buren   **D.** Wilbert Montgomery

4. Who holds the Eagles record for career receiving yards?

  A. Zach Ertz   **B.** DeSean Jackson   **C.** Pete Ratzlaff   **D.** Harold Carmichael

5. Who holds the Philadelphia record for single-season receptions?

  A. Zach Ertz   **B.** DeSean Jackson   **C.** Terrell Owens   **D.** Mike Quick

6. Which Eagles sack record is not held by Reggie White?

  A. Single-Game   **B.** Single-Season   **C.** Consecutive Games   **D.** Career

7. Which defensive back, who is also part of the three-way tie for the career record, holds the record for interceptions in a season with 11?

  A. Eric Allen   **B.** Herm Edwards   **C.** Bill Bradley   **D.** Brian Dawkins

8. What is the modern-day Eagles record for team points in a game?

  A. 57   **B.** 59   **C.** 64   **D.** 67

9. It is no surprise that Philadelphia's best regular seasons came in 2004 and 2017 when it won how many games en route to playing in the Super Bowl?

  A. 14   **B.** 13   **C.** 12   **D.** 11

10. What is the Eagles' largest comeback victory?

  A. 21 points   **B.** 22 points   **C.** 23 points   **D.** 24 points

NEW YORK GIANTS JERSEY MATH

We know everyone hates math, but we think we found a way to make it fun. Simply follow the instructions and come out with the correct number or player being hinted at.

1. The combination of Ahmad Bradshaw and Jason Sehorn results in this underrated Giants defensive lineman who anchored the unit to five NFL title game appearances in six years.

   _____

2. Multiplying Eli Manning with Tuffy Leemans allows you to find this longtime Giants running back for whom this number is retired.

   _____

3. Subtracting Mel Hein from Tiki Barber, you find the original player for whom this number was retired back in 1946.

   _____

4. Adding together Emlen Tunell and Harry Carson gives you this five-time Pro Bowl Giants linebacker from the 1990s.

   _____

5. Starting with Lawrence Taylor then subtracting Odell Beckham Jr. results in this defensive back who ranks third in team history when it comes to interceptions.

   _____

6. Double Frank Gifford and tack on a Fran Tarkenton to discover this Giants quarterback who had his number retired in 1962.

   _____

7. If you took away Victor Cruz from Amani Toomer, you'd be left with the player turned coach for whom the Giants retired this number in 1935.

   _____

8. This Giants legend is so great, he needs Ken Strong to be added to both Rodney Hampton and Jeff Hostetler.

   _____

9. The difference between Pepper Johnson and Osi Umenyiora gives you this number belonging to one of the Giants four 5,000-yard rushers.

   _____

10. Phil Simms and Jeremy Shockey come together to create this ferocious pass rusher on the Giants who did more than just nip opposing quarterbacks.

    _____

HISTORY OF THE NEW YORK GIANTS

1. Who is the Giants' all-time leading scorer?

A. Jay Feely   **B.** Lawrence Tynes   **C.** Pete Gogolak   **D.** Frank Gifford

2. Whose 513 yards against Cincinnati is the Giants record for passing yards in a game?

A. Kerry Collins   **B.** Phil Simms   **C.** Daniel Jones   **D.** Eli Manning

3. Who leads the Giants in career rushing touchdowns?

A. Brandon Jacobs   **B.** Joe Morris   **C.** Tiki Barber   **D.** Rodney Hampton

4. Who holds the Giants record for receiving yards in a season?

A. Plaxico Burress   **B.** Victor Cruz   **C.** Odell Beckham Jr.   **D.** Amani Toomer

5. Who became the first player to catch 14 passes in a game for the Giants in 2018?

A. Sterling Shepard   **B.** Odell Beckham Jr.   **C.** Evan Engram   **D.** Saquon Barkley

6. How many interceptions did Emlen Tunnell have to set the Giants record for career picks?

A. 74   **B.** 71   **C.** 68   **D.** 65

7. Who holds the Giants record for sacks in a game with six?

A. Jason Pierre-Paul   **B.** Osi Umenyiora   **C.** Justin Tuck   **D.** Michael Strahan

8. The Giants beat up the Eagles while hanging how many points on their divisional rival to set their franchise record?

A. 57   **B.** 60   **C.** 62   **D.** 64

9. On three occasions, the Giants have overcome a 20-point deficit or larger. Which of these opponents was not one of those victims?

A. Philadelphia Eagles   **B.** Indianapolis Colts   **C.** New York Jets   **D.** Arizona Cardinals

10. In which year did the Giants win a franchise-record 14 games before going on to win the Super Bowl?

A. 1986   **B.** 1990   **C.** 2007   **D.** 2011

NFC North Hunt

```
M R A L U D Z D S N O I L Z N H S
U U J S E T S R E D N A S O V I D
A Q R O D G E R S Q Z V T I N B Q
A E E F R B M D Q H Y N Y O G I K W
B L L J I M U B X A L A W L V R R Q
M O G P I G D B X P C E B E A R S
A M M B N Z N G F F T U O O V A J
L B R G N E A K R A E G I M P T O
Y A O G E C K E R A A E O R P S H
P R N R S H T Y Y C N H L N J U N
T D G G O S I B I D S T X J J T S
H I E I T I D H C R A O C J I G O
Q J C U A B C G E A Z K W O N G N
S V N O T N E K R A T R R I C C C
M V D Q Z B C B Z H E T K B H J G
O T X R F A V R E X E I Z E J E H
P C M C P V K G B D V U E J O Z P
```

KNOW YOUR DRAFT: NFC NORTH

1. Which Pro Bowl receiver did the Vikings scoop up with a fifth-round pick in 2015?

A. Cordarrelle Patterson   **B.** Adam Thielen   **C.** Stefon Diggs   **D.** Jarius Wright

2. The Packers drafted a lot of Hall-of-Famers in their early years, but which of these more recent drafts did they also pick a Hall-of-Famer?

A. 1987   **B.** 1990   **C.** 1993   **D.** 1997

3. In which year did the Bears make Brian Urlacher their first-round pick?

A. 2001   **B.** 1999   **C.** 1998   **D.** 2000

4. Which of these quarterbacks was not drafted by Detroit?

A. Otto Graham   **B.** Jack Kemp   **C.** Bobby Layne   **D.** Y.A. Tittle

5. Which of these quarterbacks was not actually drafted by the Bears?

A. Jim Harbaugh   **B.** Jim McMahon   **C.** Kyle Orton   **D.** Erik Kramer

6. Which Hall-of-Fame receiver, who never played a down in Detroit, was the Lions' third-round pick in 1965?

A. Fred Biletnikoff   **B.** Charley Taylor   **C.** Paul Warfield   **D.** John Mackey

7. Which longtime NFL receiver was a seventh-round pick by Green Bay in 1999?

A. Donald Driver   **B.** Derrick Mason   **C.** Marty Booker   **D.** Brandon Stokley

8. Which Super Bowl-winning quarterback was a ninth-round selection by Minnesota in 1992?

A. Tommy Maddox   **B.** Brad Johnson   **C.** Tony Banks   **D.** Paul Justin

9. Which of these Hall-of-Famers was not a top-five pick by the Bears?

A. Dan Hampton   **B.** Jimbo Covert   **C.** Walter Payton   **D.** Gale Sayers

10. Which of these Hall-of-Famers was not a first-round pick by the Vikings?

A. Randy Moss   **B.** Chris Doleman   **C.** Randall McDaniel   **D.** Bobby Bell

11. In which round did the Packers select Aaron Jones in the 2017 draft?

A. 2nd   **B.** 4th   **C.** 5th   **D.** 6th

12. In which round did Detroit draft its all-time leading scorer, Jason Hanson?

A. 2nd   **B.** 3rd   **C.** 5th   **D.** 6th

CHICAGO BEARS ALMA MATERS

Match the player with where he played his final season of college football before jumping to the NFL.

1. Jay Cutler		**A.** Arkansas
2. Dick Butkus		**B.** BYU
3. Matt Forte		**C.** Jackson State
4. Olin Kreutz		**D.** Louisiana
5. Walter Payton		**E.** Texas
6. Charles Tillman		**F.** Illinois
7. Jim McMahon		**G.** Washington
8. Steve McMichael		**H.** Tennessee State
9. Mike Singletary		**I.** Vanderbilt
10. Mike Ditka		**J.** Yale
11. Richard Dent		**K.** Pittsburgh
12. Dan Hampton		**L.** Arizona
13. Brian Urlacher		**M.** New Mexico
14. Gary Fencik		**N.** Baylor
15. Lance Briggs		**O.** Tulane

HISTORY OF THE CHICAGO BEARS

1. Who is the Bears' all-time leading scorer?

A. Bob Thomas   **B.** Robbie Gould   **C.** Kevin Butler   **D.** Walter Payton

2. Who holds the Bears records for most passing yards and passing touchdowns in a season?

A. Erik Kramer   **B.** Jay Cutler   **C.** Rex Grossman   **D.** Mitchell Trubisky

3. Who owns the Chicago record for rushing yards in a game with 275?

A. Thomas Jones   **B.** Gale Sayers   **C.** Walter Payton   **D.** Matt Forte

4. Who holds the Bears record for career catches?

A. Brandon Marshall   **B.** Johnny Morris   **C.** Walter Payton   **D.** Matt Forte

5. Who holds Chicago's record for receiving yards in a game?

A. Curtis Conway   **B.** Alshon Jeffrey   **C.** Brandon Marshall   **D.** Marty Booker

6. Who recently broke the Bears singles-season sack record with 18.5 sacks?

A. Akiem Hicks   **B.** Lance Briggs   **C.** Khalil Mack   **D.** Robert Quinn

7. Who tops the Bears record book with 38 career interceptions?

A. Gary Fencik   **B.** Bennie McRae   **C.** Charles Tillman   **D.** Richie Petitbon

8. Which of these Super Bowl-era records was not set by the 1985 Bears?

A. Points scored   **B.** Regular-season wins   **C.** Point differential   **D.** Points Allowed

9. How many points did the Bears score in 1965, then again in 1980 to set the franchise single-game scoring record?

A. 63   **B.** 61   **C.** 59   **D.** 57

10. How large was the Bears' record-tying comeback that led to Dennis Green's infamous rant in 2006?

A. 17 points   **B.** 20 points   **C.** 22 points   **D.** 24 points

DETROIT LIONS FAST FACTS

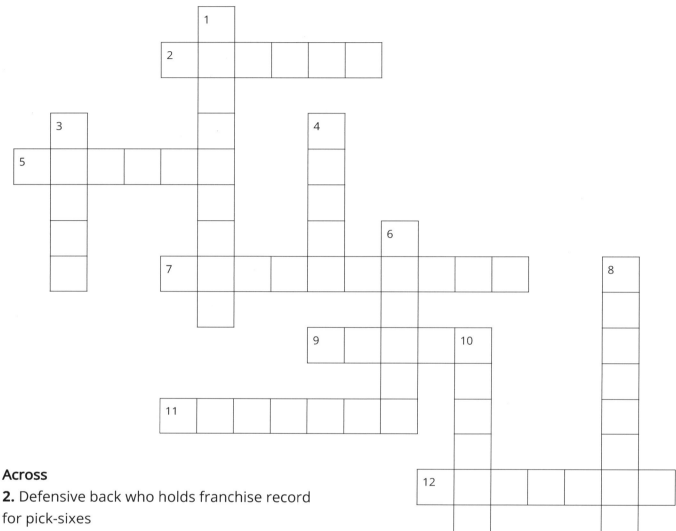

Across

2. Defensive back who holds franchise record for pick-sixes

5. Coach of Detroit's first NFL championship team

7. Ohio city from which the franchise moved to Detroit

9. Nickname of the first Lions player inducted into the Hall of Fame

11. Opponent against which Barry Sanders set franchise record with four touchdown runs

12. City where the Silverdome was located

Down

1. Book featuring George Plimpton's attempts to play quarterback at Detroit's training camp

3. Quarterback who had his records smashed by Matthew Stafford

4. Most recent receiver to catch four touchdown passes in a game

6. Only coach in Super Bowl era to be named AP Coach of the Year

8. Most recent honoree in the Pride of the Lions

10. Only player to play more than 20 years for the Lions

HISTORY OF THE DETROIT LIONS

1. Who holds the Lions record for points scored in a season?

A. Eddie Murray   **B.** Matt Prater   **C.** Jason Hanson   **D.** Barry Sanders

2. In which season did Matthew Stafford set the Lions record for passing yards and passing touchdowns in a season?

A. 2009   **B.** 2011   **C.** 2012   **D.** 2015

3. In which year did Barry Sanders set the single-season franchise record for rushing yards?

A. 1991   **B.** 1994   **C.** 1996   **D.** 1997

4. Who is barely holding onto the Lions record for catches in a season?

A. Brett Perriman   **B.** Golden Tate   **C.** Calvin Johnson   **D.** Herman Moore

5. Who leads the Lions with 109 total touchdowns scored in his career?

A. Barry Sanders   **B.** Herman Moore   **C.** Calvin Johnson   **D.** Billy Sims

6. How many interceptions did Don Doll have to set Detroit's single-game record?

A. 3   **B.** 4   **C.** 5   **D.** 6

7. Whose 95.5 official sacks are the most in Lions history?

A. William Gay   **B.** Michael Cofer   **C.** Ezekial Ansah   **D.** Robert Porcher

8. In which season did the Lions set their franchise record for points in a season?

A. 2011   **B.** 1995   **C.** 1981   **D.** 1947

9. Who was the opponent in 2013 when the Lions gained 600 yards of offense for the only time in franchise history?

A. New York Giants   **B.** Arizona Cardinals   **C.** Dallas Cowboys   **D.** Minnesota Vikings

10. What is the largest comeback victory in Lions history?

A. 21 points   **B.** 23 points   **C.** 24 points   **D.** 25 points

GREEN BAY PACKERS 3 & OUT

Can you spot the odd-man out? Three of these answers actually answer the prompt, so your job is to spot the outlier.

1. Named the Associated Press Offensive Player of the Year

A. Davante Adams   **B.** Brett Favre   **C.** Aaron Rodgers   **D.** Ahman Green

2. Has been named Coach of the Year by the Associated Press

A. Lindy Infante   **B.** Mike McCarthy   **C.** Mike Holmgren   **D.** Dan Devine

3. Did not play at least 15 seasons for the Packers

A. Bart Starr   **B.** Mason Crosby   **C.** Ray Nitschke   **D.** Donald Driver

4. Did not throw for 400 yards in a game for the Packers

A. Don Majkowski   **B.** Don Horn   **C.** Lynn Dickey   **D.** Brett Favre

5. Did not rush for 1,200 yards in a season with Green Bay

A. Dorsey Levens   **B.** Jim Taylor   **C.** Eddie Lacy   **D.** Ryan Grant

6. Did not catch at least 100 passes in a season for the Packers

A. Sterling Sharpe   **B.** Robert Brooks   **C.** Davante Adams   **D.** Jordy Nelson

7. Intercepted four passes in a game for the Packers

A. Tom Flynn   **B.** Bobby Dillon   **C.** Darren Sharper   **D.** Charles Woodson

8. Did not finish with a .600 total winning percentage as Packers coach

A. Mike Sherman   **B.** Curley Lambeau   **C.** Mike McCarthy   **D.** Mike Holmgren

9. Future NFL head coach not part of Mike Holmgren's 1992 Packers staff

A. Jon Gruden   **B.** Andy Reid   **C.** Marty Mornhinweg   **D.** Dick Jauron

10. Not a year in which the Packers held a stock drive

A. 1950   **B.** 1996   **C.** 2011   **D.** 2021

HISTORY OF THE GREEN BAY PACKERS

1. Who is the Packers' all-time leading scorer?

A. Don Hutson **B.** Ryan Longwell **C.** Paul Hornung **D.** Mason Crosby

2. In which year did Aaron Rodgers set the Green Bay single-season passing record?

A. 2011 **B.** 2016 **C.** 2018 **D.** 2020

3. Who holds the Packers record for most rushing yards in a season?

A. Dorsey Levens **B.** Ryan Grant **C.** Ahman Green **D.** Jim Taylor

4. Whose 19 rushing touchdowns is the high mark for the Packers in a single season?

A. Paul Hornung **B.** Dorsey Levens **C.** Jim Taylor **D.** Aaron Jones

5. Who leads the Packers in career receiving yards?

A. Davante Adams **B.** James Lofton **C.** Sterling Sharpe **D.** Donald Driver

6. Who holds the Packers record for career sacks?

A. Kabeer Gbaja-Biamila **B.** Clay Matthews **C.** Vonnie Holliday **D.** Reggie White

7. Who is the only player in Packers history to intercept 10 passes in a season?

A. Irv Comp **B.** Bobby Dillon **C.** Charles Woodson **D.** Willie Wood

8. In 2011, the Packers set their franchise record with 15 wins, but how many games did they win in a row to start the season, another franchise record?

A. 13 **B.** 12 **C.** 11 **D.** 10

9. What is the largest deficit Green Bay has overcome to win a game?

A. 20 points **B.** 22 points **C.** 23 points **D.** 25 points

10. Twice in 1962 the Packers posted identical scorelines for their largest victory in franchise history. What was that score?

A. 48-0 **B.** 49-0 **C.** 52-0 **D.** 54-0

MINNESOTA VIKINGS JERSEY MATH

We know everyone hates math, but we think we found a way to make it fun. Simply follow the instructions and come out with the correct number or player being hinted at.

1. Kirk Cousins added to Steve Hutchinson results in this Hall-of-Fame receiver who is could rise to the moon to catch a pass.

_____

2. Justin Jefferson is subtracted from Bryant McKinnie to get a Hall-of-Fame pass rusher.

_____

3. Even after multiplying Blair Walsh by Fred Cox, you're still an Ahmad Rashad short of the defensive lineman who has played more games for the Vikings than any other player in team history.

_____

4. When added together, Scott Studwell and Paul Krause result in a Vikings Ring of Honor member who died on the field.

_____

5. Antoine Winfield is doubled, then an extra point is added to get this longtime Vikings center who has played more games than any other offensive player in team history.

_____

6. Jared Allen stopped chasing Daunte Culpepper long enough to join forces, resulting in this legendary receiver with the same initials for his first and last name.

_____

7. Gary Zimmerman and Adrian Peterson combine to get this Hall-of-Famer who rushed the passer for most of his legendary career in Minnesota.

_____

8. This Vikings Ring of Honor offensive lineman results from Kyle Rudolph combining with Gary Andersen, but then having Fran Tarkenton subtracted from the total.

_____

9. Everson Griffen subtracts Dalvin Cook with a blitz and it results in this legendary guard blocking the way for Minnesota.

_____

10. Add together Randall Cunningham and Carl Eller to find the verdict on this Vikings defensive lineman.

_____

HISTORY OF THE MINNESOTA VIKINGS

1. Who is Minnesota's all-time leading scorer?

A. Blair Walsh　　　　**B.** Gary Andersen　　　　**C.** Fred Cox　　　　**D.** Cris Carter

2. Who holds the Vikings record for most passing yards in a season?

A. Daunte Culpepper　　**B.** Sam Bradford　　**C.** Kirk Cousins　　**D.** Randall Cunningham

3. Adrian Peterson has the top five games with the most rushing yards in Vikings history. Who has the sixth?

A. Chuck Foreman　　**B.** Michael Bennett　　**C.** Robert Smith　　**D.** Dalvin Cook

4. Who holds the Vikings record for catches in a season?

A. Sammy White　　**B.** Randy Moss　　**C.** Cris Carter　　**D.** Adam Thielen

5. Who holds the Vikings record for receiving yards in a season?

A. Sammy White　　**B.** Randy Moss　　**C.** Cris Carter　　**D.** Justin Jefferson

6. Who holds the Vikings record for career interceptions with 53 picks?

A. Paul Krause　　**B.** Bobby Bryant　　**C.** Antoine Winfield　　**D.** Joey Browner

7. In 2011, Jared Allen set the franchise record for sacks in a season with how many quarterback takedowns?

A. 22　　　　**B.** 21.5　　　　**C.** 21　　　　**D.** 20

8. What is the Vikings record for most team points scored in a game?

A. 61　　　　**B.** 58　　　　**C.** 56　　　　**D.** 54

9. How large was the margin in Minnesota's biggest victory in franchise history?

A. 45 points　　**B.** 47 points　　**C.** 48 points　　**D.** 51 points

10. What deficit did the Vikings overcome in 1977 against San Francisco for the largest comeback win in franchise history?

A. 24 points　　**B.** 23 points　　**C.** 21 points　　**D.** 20 points

NFC South Hunt

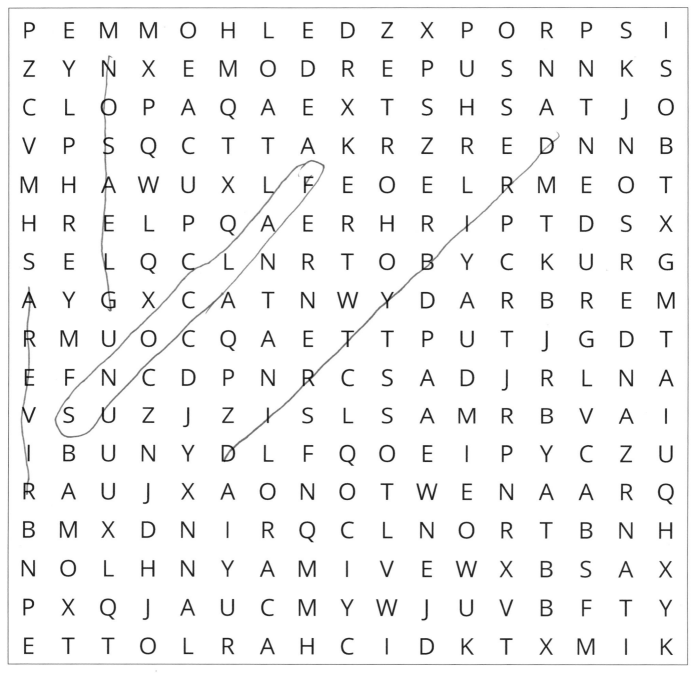

P	E	M	M	O	H	L	E	D	Z	X	P	O	R	P	S	I
Z	Y	N	X	E	M	O	D	R	E	P	U	S	N	N	K	S
C	L	O	P	A	Q	A	E	X	T	S	H	S	A	T	J	O
V	P	S	Q	C	T	T	A	K	R	Z	R	E	D	N	N	B
M	H	A	W	U	X	L	F	E	O	E	L	R	M	E	O	T
H	R	E	L	P	Q	A	E	R	H	R	I	P	T	D	S	X
S	E	L	Q	C	L	N	R	T	O	B	Y	C	K	U	R	G
A	Y	G	X	C	A	T	N	W	Y	D	A	R	B	R	E	M
R	M	U	O	C	Q	A	E	T	T	P	U	T	J	G	D	T
E	F	N	C	D	P	N	R	C	S	A	D	J	R	L	N	A
V	S	U	Z	J	Z	I	S	L	S	A	M	R	B	V	A	I
I	B	U	N	Y	D	L	F	Q	O	E	I	P	Y	C	Z	U
R	A	U	J	X	A	O	N	O	T	W	E	N	A	A	R	Q
B	M	X	D	N	I	R	Q	C	L	N	O	R	T	B	N	H
N	O	L	H	N	Y	A	M	I	V	E	W	X	B	S	A	X
P	X	Q	J	A	U	C	M	Y	W	J	U	V	B	F	T	Y
E	T	T	O	L	R	A	H	C	I	D	K	T	X	M	I	K

Anderson	Delhomme	Panthers
Atlanta	Dirty Bird	Rivera
Brady	Falcons	Ryan
Brees	Gleason	Saints
Buccaneers	Gruden	Superdome
Carolina	New Orleans	Tampa Bay
Charlotte	Newton	

KNOW YOUR DRAFT: NFC SOUTH

1. Which defensive back did the Panthers find in the fifth round of the 2012 draft?

A. Tre Boston   **B.** Josh Norman   **C.** Richard Sherman   **D.** Captain Munnerlyn

2. Who was not a quarterback taken by the Buccaneers in the first round?

A. Trent Dilfer   **B.** Doug Williams   **C.** Shaun King   **D.** Josh Freeman

3. In which year did the Saints not draft a Hall-of-Famer?

A. 1981   **B.** 1982   **C.** 1993   **D.** 1994

4. Which future NFL starter did the Falcons draft in the third round in 2004?

A. Seneca Wallace   **B.** Matt Cassel   **C.** Luke McCown   **D.** Matt Schaub

5. Which defensive back did the Buccaneers manage to find in the third round of the 1997 draft?

A. Ronde Barber   **B.** Donnie Abraham   **C.** John Lynch   **D.** Deshea Townsend

6. Which tight end did the Saints draft in the third round in 2010?

A. Kyle Rudolph   **B.** Jimmy Graham   **C.** Jared Cook   **D.** Dennis Pitta

7. Which franchise running back did the Falcons draft with the 201st overall pick?

A. William Andrews   **B.** Jamal Anderson   **C.** Warrick Dunn   **D.** Gerald Riggs

8. Who was not a top-10 draft pick by Carolina?

A. Luke Kuechly   **B.** Kerry Collins   **C.** Thomas Davis   **D.** Julius Peppers

9. In which year did the Buccaneers land their dynamic defensive duo of Derrick Brooks and Warren Sapp in the first round?

A. 1994   **B.** 1996   **C.** 1997   **D.** 1995

10. In which round of the 2001 NFL Draft did the Panthers select Steve Smith?

A. 3rd   **B.** 4th   **C.** 5th   **D.** 7th

11. Which of these players was not drafted by Atlanta with the No. 1 overall pick?

A. Steve Bartkowski   **B.** Tony Casillas   **C.** Aundray Bruce   **D.** Michael Vick

12. Which of these Pro Bowl quarterbacks was actually drafted by New Orleans?

A. Marc Bulger   **B.** Matt Hasselbeck   **C.** Jeff Garcia   **D.** Jake Plummer

TAMPA BAY BUCCANEERS FAST FACTS

Across

4. Nickname of Buccaneers' most recent Offensive Rookie of the Year

7. Nickname given to Tampa Stadium

9. Team Tampa Bay defeated for first regular season win

10. Original owner of franchise

11. Landmark where Buccaneers held training camp from 2002-08

12. First jersey retired in team history honored this man

Down

1. Title given to Buccaneers' pirate mascot

2. First coach in team history

3. Only player with 2,000 yards from scrimmage in a season

5. Holds team record for most Pro Bowl appearances

6. Nickname for the franchise's orange uniforms

8. One of two players to play at least 200 games for the Buccaneers

HISTORY OF THE TAMPA BAY BUCCANEERS

1. Who is the Buccaneers' all-time leading scorer?

A. Martin Gramatica   **B.** Mike Evans   **C.** Connor Barth   **D.** Michael Husted

2. Who holds the Tampa Bay record for most career passing yards?

A. Tom Brady   **B.** Vinny Testaverde   **C.** Brad Johnson   **D.** Jameis Winston

3. Who is the only Buccaneers running back to rush for 1,500 yards in a season?

A. Carnell Williams   **B.** Doug Martin   **C.** Warrick Dunn   **D.** James Wilder

4. Who is the only Tampa Bay receiver to catch 100 passes in a season?

A. Keyshawn Johnson   **B.** Keenan McCardell   **C.** Mike Evans   **D.** Chris Godwin

5. Who has scored the most touchdowns in Buccaneers history?

A. Mike Alstott   **B.** James Wilder   **C.** Mike Evans   **D.** Warrick Dunn

6. Who holds the Buccaneers' record for most sacks in franchise history?

A. Warren Sapp   **B.** Lee Roy Selmon   **C.** Gerald McCoy   **D.** Simeon Rice

7. Which defensive back intercepted 10 passes to set the franchise record for interceptions in a season?

A. Aqib Talib   **B.** Ronde Barber   **C.** Cedric Brown   **D.** John Lynch

8. The only time Tampa Bay has rallied from a 20-point deficit came in 2008 when the Buccaneers overcame a 21-point deficit to defeat which team?

A. Carolina Panthers   **B.** Atlanta Falcons   **C.** Kansas City Chiefs   **D.** Denver Broncos

9. From 2018-2021, the Buccaneers set and then broke the team season scoring record. Which year held the record prior to this streak?

A. 2012   **B.** 2008   **C.** 2004   **D.** 2002

10. What is the most points Tampa Bay has scored in a single game?

A. 62   **B.** 59   **C.** 57   **D.** 55

ATLANTA FALCONS 3 & OUT

Can you spot the odd-man out? Three of these answers actually answer the prompt, so your job is to spot the outlier.

1. A member of the Falcons Ring of Honor

A. Warrick Dunn   **B.** Jamal Anderson   **C.** Tommy Nobis   **D.** Mike Kenn

2. Played at least 12 seasons for the Falcons

A. Tommy Nobis   **B.** Mike Kenn   **C.** Jeff Van Note   **D.** Matt Ryan

3. Caught at least 100 passes in a season for the Falcons

A. Roddy White   **B.** Terance Mathis   **C.** Julio Jones   **D.** Tony Gonzalez

4. Did not throw for 4,000 yards in a season for Atlanta

A. Steve Bartkowski   **B.** Matt Schaub   **C.** Jeff George   **D.** Chris Chandler

5. Did not return at least two kickoffs for a touchdown

A. Deion Sanders   **B.** Eric Weems   **C.** Allen Rossum   **D.** Tim Dwight

6. Registered at least five sacks in a game for the Falcons

A. Claude Humphrey   **B.** John Abraham   **C.** Chuck Smith   **D.** Adrian Clayborn

7. Won 40 games as Falcons coach

A. Dan Quinn   **B.** Norm Van Brocklin   **C.** Dan Reeves   **D.** Leeman Bennett

8. Didn't win 20 games as the Falcons starter

A. Bob Berry   **B.** Jeff George   **C.** Matt Schaub   **D.** Chris Miller

9. Named to five Pro Bowls with Atlanta

A. Jessie Tuggle   **B.** Keith Brooking   **C.** Alge Crumpler   **D.** George Kunz

10. A principal owner for the Falcons at some point

A. Arthur Blank   **B.** Rankin Smith Sr.   **C.** Dorothy Smith Knox   **D.** Taylor Smith

HISTORY OF THE ATLANTA FALCONS

1. Who is Atlanta's all-time leading scorer?

A. Jay Feely   **B.** Morten Andersen   **C.** William Andrews   **D.** Matt Bryant

2. Who holds the Falcons record for most completions in a game?

A. Steve Bartkowski   **B.** Matt Ryan   **C.** Matt Schaub   **D.** Chris Chandler

3. Whose 220-yard performance is the high mark for Falcons rushers in a game?

A. Jamal Anderson   **B.** Michael Turner   **C.** Warrick Dunn   **D.** Michael Vick

4. Who holds the Falcons record for most career rushing yards?

A. Gerald Riggs   **B.** Michael Turner   **C.** Jamal Anderson   **D.** William Andrews

5. Which of Julio Jones' totals is the Atlanta record for most receiving yards in a season?

A. 2015   **B.** 2014   **C.** 2018   **D.** 2016

6. Who do the Falcons credit as their all-time sacks leader?

A. Tommy Nobis   **B.** Claude Humphrey   **C.** John Abraham   **D.** Chuck Smith

7. Who holds the Falcons record with 39 career interceptions?

A. Scott Case   **B.** Rolland Lawrence   **C.** DeAngelo Hall   **D.** Ray Brown

8. In 1973, Atlanta set the franchise record for largest victory when they defeated New Orleans by how much?

A. 46 points   **B.** 49 points   **C.** 51 points   **D.** 55 points

9. In which season did the Falcons set their franchise record for points in a season?

A. 1981   **B.** 1998   **C.** 2016   **D.** 2017

10. Within a month of each other, Atlanta set then tied its record for largest comeback win by rallying back from how large of a deficit?

A. 27 points   **B.** 24 points   **C.** 23 points   **D.** 21 points

CAROLINA PANTHERS JERSEY MATH

We know everyone hates math, but we think we found a way to make it fun. Simply follow the instructions and come out with the correct number or player being hinted at.

1. You were trying to double DeAngelo Williams, but missed the extra point and ended up with this longtime Panthers center.

   _____

2. When combining Mike Minter and Jonathan Stewart, the result is this Carolina linebacker who has played more playoff games than any other Panthers player.

   _____

3. Multiplying Christian McCaffrey and John Kasay will get you this Panthers tight end who became a fan favorite during his time with Carolina.

   _____

4. All it takes to find this risky Carolina defensive back is to subtract Kris Jenkins from Mario Addison.

   _____

5. Adding Robby Anderson and Kelvin Benjamin would create this nightmare for receivers who found his star power in Carolina's secondary for the 2015 Super Bowl squad.

   _____

6. It only takes an additional D.J. Moore to get from Muhsin Muhammed to the greatest receiver in team history, who played more than 180 games for the franchise.

   _____

7. By multiplying Derek Anderson and Jake Delhomme you get the latest in a long line of excellent linebackers for the Panthers defense.

   _____

8. If you tried to divide Wesley Walls by Kerry Collins, you'd get this number worn by Jason Baker with an extra Cam Newton left over.

   _____

9. Subtracting Luke Kuechly from Julius Peppers, you don't get any better at defense, but you do get this number that was worn by Richard Marshall for his five years in Carolina.

   _____

10. When Anthony Johnson and Travelle Wharton end up in a dogpile together, they combine and the result is this Panthers defensive end who twice put up double-digit sacks in nine years with the team.

   _____

HISTORY OF THE CAROLINA PANTHERS

1. Who is the Panthers' all-time leading scorer?

A. Cam Newton   **B.** John Kasay   **C.** Steve Smith   **D.** Graham Gano

2. Who is atop the Panthers record book for single-season passing yards?

A. Steve Beuerlein   **B.** Cam Newton   **C.** Kerry Collins   **D.** Jake Delhomme

3. Who holds the Panthers single-game record with four rushing touchdowns?

A. Stephen Davis   **B.** Jonathan Stewart   **C.** DeAngelo Williams   **D.** Cam Newton

4. Who holds the Carolina record for the most rushing yards in a season?

A. Jonathan Stewart   **B.** Christian McCaffrey   **C.** Stephen Davis   **D.** DeAngelo Williams

5. Who is the only Panthers receiver to go over 200 receiving yards in a game?

A. Steve Smith   **B.** Muhsin Muhammed   **C.** Greg Olsen   **D.** Kelvin Benjamin

6. Who holds the Panthers record for most career interceptions?

A. Eric Davis   **B.** Josh Norman   **C.** Doug Evans   **D.** Chris Gamble

7. Who shares Carolina's single-season sack record with Greg Hardy?

A. Mike Rucker   **B.** Julius Peppers   **C.** Charles Johnson   **D.** Kevin Greene

8. Who did Carolina defeat when it scored 50 points in a game for the only time in franchise history?

A. New York Giants   **B.** New York Jets   **C.** Cincinnati Bengals   **D.** Cleveland Browns

9. How many consecutive games did Carolina win to start the 2015 season?

A. 15   **B.** 14   **C.** 13   **D.** 12

10. What is the largest comeback victory for the Panthers franchise?

A. 17 points   **B.** 20 points   **C.** 21 points   **D.** 23 points

NEW ORLEANS SAINTS ALMA MATERS

Match the player with where he played his final season of college football before jumping to the NFL.

1. Aaron Brooks	**A.** Illinois
2. Will Smith	**B.** Purdue
3. Marques Colston	**C.** Colorado
4. Alvin Kamara	**D.** Ohio State
5. Rickey Jackson	**E.** Louisiana Tech
6. Jahri Evans	**F.** Hofstra
7. Pat Swilling	**G.** Tennessee
8. Pierre Thomas	**H.** Mississippi
9. Drew Brees	**I.** Pittsburgh
10. Stan Brock	**J.** Notre Dame
11. Cameron Jordan	**K.** LSU
12. Eric Martin	**L.** Virginia
13. Deuce McAllister	**M.** California
14. Dave Waymer	**N.** Bloomsburg
15. Willie Roaf	**O.** Georgia Tech

HISTORY OF THE NEW ORLEANS SAINTS

1. Who is the all-time leading scorer in Saints history?

A. Will Lutz **B.** Morten Andersen **C.** Alvin Kamara **D.** John Carney

2. What is Drew Brees' record for most passing touchdowns in a game?

A. 5 **B.** 6 **C.** 7 **D.** 8.

3. Who holds the New Orleans record for rushing yards in a game and in a season?

A. George Rogers **B.** Mark Ingram **C.** Rueben Mayes **D.** Deuce McAllister

4. Who now holds the Saints record for receiving yards in a game?

A. Michael Thomas **B.** Eric Martin **C.** Wes Chandler **D.** Joe Horn

5. Who holds the Saints record for most touchdowns scored?

A. Mark Ingram **B.** Alvin Kamara **C.** Deuce McAllister **D.** Marques Colston

6. Who holds the New Orleans record for most career sacks?

A. Cameron Jordan **B.** Wayne Martin **C.** Rickey Jackson **D.** Will Smith

7. Which defensive back holds the Saints record for career interceptions?

A. Tommy Myers **B.** Dave Waymer **C.** Dave Whitsell **D.** Sammy Knight

8. In which season did the Raiders set their franchise record for points in a season?

A. 2014 **B.** 2018 **C.** 2009 **D.** 2011

9. How many points did New Orleans score in 2011 against the Colts to set the franchise's single-game scoring record?

A. 62 **B.** 58 **C.** 55 **D.** 53

10. What is the largest comeback victory for the Saints franchise?

A. 21 points **B.** 22 points **C.** 23 points **D.** 24 points

NFC West Hunt

```
G Q G D F Q C V E H A V Z E N T J
S S K K M X G C E O H G N U O Y S
Z X R T F S R H W A R N E R V L M U
Y Q T E M O M D J R M P N C A H J
T T O L N B W O M L R E E R W E O
T E B H G I W O P A I O I A I C S
S A N F R A N C I S C O L L Z I M
E Q Y T M T W K T Q Z S D L S R V
A Z S L A Z T L Q D H U S E S S G
H H L N O D W U E S A I L E J K K
A D A U I R H A I A U E A T Y D I
W E N B U Y B F N O G T U Q M S L
K E I B W J I O L N T K D Q R E S
S D D H G N Z T A L N Q Y E V P O
P H R O Z I S S E B D D V D I K N
Y E A H R Y O D L A R E G Z T I F
Q E C A W L W Z F T W O E K M Q O
```

Arizona	Montana	St. Louis
Cardinals	Niners	Vermeil
Carroll	Rams	Walsh
Faulk	Rice	Warner
Fitzgerald	San Francisco	Wilson
Los Angeles	Seahawks	Young
Lott	Seattle	

KNOW YOUR DRAFT: NFC WEST

1. Which Heisman Trophy winner was drafted by San Francisco before turning to coaching?

A. Johnny Lujack

B. Steve Spurrier

C. John David Crow

D. Vic Janowicz

2. Which Hall-of-Famer was a third-round pick of the Cardinals in 1991?

A. Aenas Williams

B. Ricky Watters

C. Will Shields

D. Ed McCaffrey

3. Which running back was actually a third-round pick by the Seahawks before blossoming elsewhere?

A. Sammy Winder

B. Ahman Green

C. DeShaun Foster

D. Charlie Garner

4. In which round did the Rams end up drafting Deacon Jones in 1961?

A. 11th

B. 12th

C. 13th

D. 14th

5. Which receiver did the 49ers draft in the 10th round of the 1979 draft?

A. Ken MacAfee

B. Drew Hill

C. Mike Shumann

D. Dwight Clark

6. The magic is alive and well for the Rams, who drafted Ryan Fitzpatrick in the seventh round in which year?

A. 2003

B. 2004

C. 2005

D. 2006

7. Which kicker was drafted by Seattle then spent 20 years in the NFL, playing in more than 300 games?

A. Josh Brown

B. John Kasay

C. Norm Johnson

D. Rian Lindell

8. Arizona picked this running back in the fifth round in 1990, but he ended up with more catches than rushing attempts for the Cardinals.

A. Garrison Hearst

B. Johnny Johnson

C. Larry Centers

D. Anthony Thompson

9. Which of these Hall-of-Fame offensive linemen was not drafted by Seattle?

A. Larry Allen

B. Walter Jones

C. Kevin Mawae

D. Steve Hutchinson

10. Which of these receivers drafted by the Rams was not a first-round pick?

A. Isaac Bruce

B. Eddie Kennison

C. Torry Holt

D. Elroy Hirsch

11. Frank Gore ended his career as the NFL's third-leading rusher, but in which round did the 49ers start his career by drafting him?

A. 1st

B. 2nd

C. 3rd

D. 4th

12. Tom Tupa was Arizona's third-round pick in 1988, but which position did the Cardinals draft him to play?

A. Safety

B. Quarterback

C. Kicker

D. Punter

SAN FRANCISCO 49ERS ALMA MATERS

Match the player with where he played his final season of college football before jumping to the NFL.

1. Jimmy Johnson

A. Notre Dame

2. Roger Craig

B. Central Michigan

3. Joe Montana

C. BYU

4. Garrison Hearst

D. USC

5. Leo Nomellini

E. Mississippi Valley State

6. Jesse Sapolu

F. Nebraska

7. Jerry Rice

G. Georgia

8. Patrick Willis

H. Minnesota

9. Joe Staley

I. Stanford

10. Steve Young

J. Clemson

11. Dwight Clark

K. Washington

12. Hugh McElhenny

L. UCLA

13. Ronnie Lott

M. Hawaii

14. John Brodie

N. UT-Chattanooga

15. Terrell Owens

O. Mississippi

HISTORY OF THE SAN FRANCISCO 49ERS

1. Who is San Francisco's all-time leading scorer?

A. Mike Cofer
B. Robbie Gould
C. Jerry Rice
D. Ray Wersching

2. Who holds the 49ers record for most passing yards in a season?

A. Jeff Garcia
B. Jimmy Garoppolo
C. Ken Stabler
D. Steve Young

3. Who sits atop the 49ers record book for most rushing yards in a season?

A. Joe Perry
B. Frank Gore
C. Garrison Hearst
D. Ricky Watters

4. One of the few records Jerry Rice does not hold, who has the most catches in a game in 49ers history?

A. John Taylor
B. Dwight Clark
C. George Kittle
D. Terrell Owens

5. In which year did Jerry Rice set the single-season record for receiving yards?

A. 1986
B. 1990
C. 1993
D. 1995

6. Who holds the 49ers record for most career sacks?

A. Aldon Smith
B. Bryant Young
C. Dana Stubblefield
D. Charles Haley

7. Which of these interception records does not belong to Ronnie Lott in some capacity?

A. Single game
B. Career
C. Single season
D. Career touchdowns

8. What is the 49ers franchise record for team points scored in a game?

A. 56
B. 59
C. 62
D. 65

9. How big was the largest win in San Francisco's history back in 1961 against the Lions?

A. 42 points
B. 45 points
C. 49 points
D. 52 points

10. What is the largest comeback victory for the Raiders franchise?

A. 30 points
B. 28 points
C. 27 points
D. 24 points

ARIZONA CARDINALS JERSEY MATH

We know everyone hates math, but we think we found a way to make it fun. Simply follow the instructions and come out with the correct number or player being hinted at.

1. This Hall-of-Fame offensive lineman is the result of adding Pat Tillman to Tyran Mathieu.

_____

2. Jake Plummer and J.J. Arrington are added together to get this Heisman Trophy winning running back who finished third in MVP voting in 1960.

_____

3. If Roger Wehrli is subtracted from Stan Mauldin, the result is this Cardinals pass rusher who holds the franchise record for career sacks.

_____

4. Carson Palmer multiplied by Larry Fitzgerald results in this Hall-of-Fame running back.

_____

5. If you took Stump Mitchell away from Cedric Mack, you'd be left with the Cardinals' all-time leader in passing yards.

_____

6. Larry Stallings and Ottis Anderson are added together, and the result is this running back who has his number retired by the franchise.

_____

7. Subtracting Kyler Murray from Budda Baker gives you another Cardinals defensive back; this one, though, is in the Hall of Fame.

_____

8. When J.V. Cain is divided by Larry Wilson, you get this receiver who has re-written the Cardinals record book.

_____

9. Tack on a field goal to Anquan Boldin, then divide him by Jay Feely at the end of his Cardinals career to get this defensive back who tied the NFL record for punt return touchdowns in a season.

_____

10. The difference between Karlos Dansby's two numbers with the Cardinals is the same number worn by Charley Trippi during his two Pro Bowl seasons.

_____

HISTORY OF THE ARIZONA CARDINALS

1. Who is the Cardinals' all-time leading scorer?

A. Neil Rackers   **B.** Jim Bakken   **C.** Greg Davis   **D.** Larry Fitzgerald

2. Who holds the Cardinals record for most career passing yards?

A. Jake Plummer   **B.** Neil Lomax   **C.** Kurt Warner   **D.** Jim Hart

3. Who is the only Cardinals running back to rush for 1,300 yards in a season?

A. Ottis Anderson   **B.** Jim Otis   **C.** Edgerrin James   **D.** David Johnson

4. Who holds the Arizona record for rushing yards in a game?

A. Ottis Anderson   **B.** David Johnson   **C.** Beanie Wells   **D.** John David Crow

5. Larry Fitzgerlad is the clear leader for career receiving yards, but who holds the Arizona record for receiving yards in a season?

A. Rob Moore   **B.** Roy Green   **C.** David Boston   **D.** Anquan Boldin

6. Who set the Cardinals record for career interceptions with 52 picks?

A. Roger Wehrli   **B.** Larry Wilson   **C.** Aenas Williams   **D.** Bob Nussbaumer

7. Who leads the Cardinals in career sacks and holds the single-season record?

A. Simeon Rice   **B.** Curtis Greer   **C.** Calais Campbell   **D.** Chandler Jones

8. In which season did Arizona set the franchise record for regular-season wins?

A. 2015   **B.** 2014   **C.** 2012   **D.** 2008

9. Who did the Cardinals play in 1996 when they gained 600 yards in a game for the only time in franchise history?

A. Washington Commanders   **B.** New York Giants   **C.** Dallas Cowboys   **D.** Philadelphia Eagles

10. What is the largest comeback victory in the vast history of the Cardinals?

A. 27 points   **B.** 25 points   **C.** 23 points   **D.** 21 points

LOS ANGELES RAMS FAST FACTS

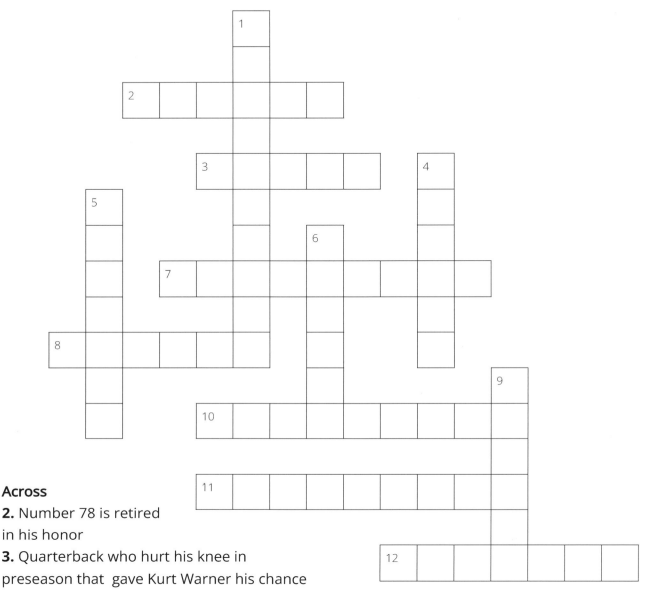

Across

2. Number 78 is retired in his honor

3. Quarterback who hurt his knee in preseason that gave Kurt Warner his chance

7. City from which the team moved to Los Angeles the first time

8. Receiver Isaac Bruce and Torry Holt passed on all-time yards list

10. Owner when Rams won Super Bowl for first time

11. Los Angeles County city where SoFi Stadium is located

12. Only player not named Eric Dickerson to rush for 1500 yards in a season

Down

1. First Rams player inducted into Hall of Fame

4. Franchise's most recent AP NFL MVP

5. Future NFL commissioner who began career with Rams

6. Nickname by which most people know David Jones

9. First coach in team history

HISTORY OF THE LOS ANGELES RAMS

1. Who is the Rams' all-time leading scorer?

A. Mike Lansford   **B.** Greg Zuerlein   **C.** Marshall Faulk   **D.** Jeff Wilkins

2. Who holds the Rams record for most career passing yards?

A. Roman Gabriel   **B.** Kurt Warner   **C.** Jim Everett   **D.** Marc Bulger

3. Who is the Rams' all-time leading rusher?

A. Eric Dickerson   **B.** Steven Jackson   **C.** Marshall Faulk   **D.** Tom Wilson

4. Who leads the Rams in career receiving yards?

A. Henry Ellard   **B.** Isaac Bruce   **C.** Cooper Kupp   **D.** Torry Holt

5. Who holds the Rams record for most touchdowns scored in their career?

A. Marshall Faulk   **B.** Isaac Bruce   **C.** Eric Dickerson   **D.** Torry Holt

6. Who holds the record for most sacks by a Rams defender in a season since sacks became an official statistic?

A. Aaron Donald   **B.** Gary Jeter   **C.** Robert Quinn   **D.** Kevin Greene

7. Which defensive back recorded 46 interceptions to set the Rams career record?

A. Nolan Cromwell   **B.** LeRoy Irvin   **C.** Dick Lane   **D.** Ed Meador

8. What is the Rams record for most team points scored in a game?

A. 65   **B.** 67   **C.** 70   **D.** 71

9. Which team record is not held by the 2000 Rams?

A. Most points allowed   **B.** Most points scored   **C.** Most first downs   **D.** Most yards gained

10. What is the largest comeback victory for the Rams franchise?

A. 28 points   **B.** 24 points   **C.** 21 points   **D.** 19 points

SEATTLE SEAHAWKS 3 & OUT

Can you spot the odd-man out? Three of these answers actually answer the prompt, so your job is to spot the outlier.

1. A member of the Seahawks Ring of Honor

A. Kenny Easley   **B.** Dave Kreig   **C.** Shaun Alexander   **D.** Paul Allen

2. Named Associated Press Offensive or Defensive Player of the Year

A. Russell Wilson   **B.** Shaun Alexander   **C.** Kenny Easley   **D.** Cortez Kennedy

3. Played at least 200 games for the Seahawks

A. Steve Largent   **B.** Walter Jones   **C.** Mack Strong   **D.** Joe Nash

4. Threw for 400 yards in a game for the Seahawks

A. Jim Zorn   **B.** Matt Hasselbeck   **C.** Dave Kreig   **D.** Warren Moon

5. Ran for 200 yards in a game with Seattle

A. Shaun Alexander   **B.** Thomas Rawls   **C.** Curt Warner   **D.** Marshawn Lynch

6. Caught at least 90 passes in a season for the Seahawks

A. Tyler Lockett   **B.** Doug Baldwin   **C.** Steve Largent   **D.** Bobby Engram

7. Holds a share of the Seahawks record with three interceptions in a game

A. Marcus Trufant   **B.** Shawn Springs   **C.** Eugene Robinson   **D.** Lofa Tatupu

8. Returned both a punt and kickoff for a touchdown with Seattle

A. Charlie Rogers   **B.** Leon Washington   **C.** Nate Burleson   **D.** Tyler Lockett

9. Held the title of executive vice president or president with the Seahawks

A. Pete Carroll   **B.** Tom Flores   **C.** Mike Holmgren   **D.** Chuck Knox

10. Hall of Famer who finished his career in Seattle

A. Warren Moon   **B.** John Randle   **C.** Franco Harris   **D.** Jerry Rice

HISTORY OF THE SEATTLE SEAHAWKS

1. Who is Seattle's all-time leading scorer?

A. Norm Johnson   **B.** Shaun Alexander   **C.** Josh Brown   **D.** Steven Hauschka

2. Who set the Seahawks' standard with 452 passing yards in a game against Houston?

A. Jim Zorn   **B.** Russell Wilson   **C.** Seneca Wallace   **D.** Matt Hasselbeck

3. Who holds the Seahawks record for career rushing yards?

A. Marshawn Lynch   **B.** Thomas Rawls   **C.** Curt Warner   **D.** Shaun Alexander

4. Who is the only Seattle receiver to eclipse 1,300 receiving yards in a season?

A. D.K. Metcalf   **B.** Brian Blades   **C.** Steve Largent   **D.** Doug Baldwin

5. In which season did Shaun Alexander set the then-NFL record with 28 touchdowns in a season?

A. 2003   **B.** 2004   **C.** 2005   **D.** 2006

6. Who holds the Seahawks record for most sacks in a season?

A. Cortez Kennedy   **B.** Jeff Bryant   **C.** Michael Sinclair   **D.** Jacob Green

7. Who leads the Seahawks with 50 career interceptions for the franchise?

A. Kenny Easley   **B.** Dave Brown   **C.** Eugene Robinson   **D.** Richard Sherman

8. In which season did Seattle set its franchise record for wins in a season?

A. 2020   **B.** 2014   **C.** 2012   **D.** 2005

9. Who was the opponent when the Seahawks rallied from a 21-0 deficit for the largest comeback win in franchise history?

A. Chicago Bears   **B.** Arizona Cardinals   **C.** San Francisco 49ers   **D.** Tampa Bay Buccaneers

10. What is the most points the Seahawks have scored in a game in franchise history?

A. 58   **B.** 56   **C.** 54   **D.** 51

CHAPTER

4

FOURTH DOWN
Record Book

Super Bowl
LOCATION, LOCATION, LOCATION

Can you guess how many Super Bowls each city marked on this map has hosted?

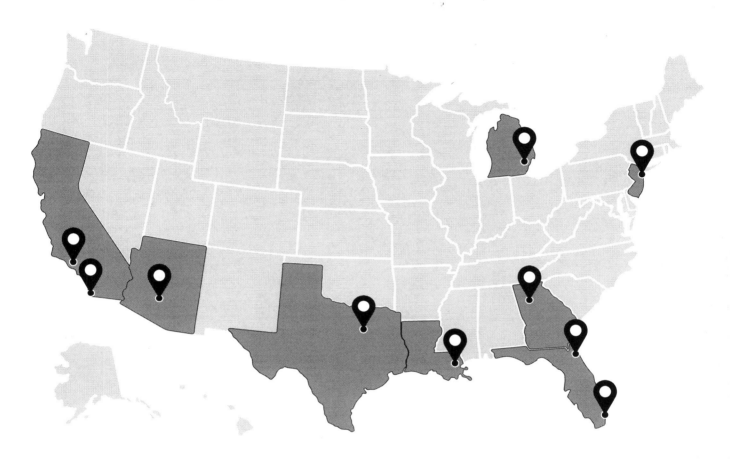

Miami	_____	Indianapolis	_____
Jacksonville	_____	New York City	_____
Dallas	_____	New Orleans	_____
Los Angeles	_____	Tampa	_____
Phoenix	_____	Atlanta	_____
Houston	_____	San Diego	_____
Detroit	_____	Minneapolis	_____
San Francisco	_____		

VISITING THE MOUSE

The beauty of the Super Bowl is that it is an opportunity for unheralded stars to step up and make a big difference for their team. Everyone knows the legends who have been named MVP of the biggest game, but what about these 12 faces of other past Super Bowl MVPs?

1 _____ 2 _____ 3 _____

4 _____ 5 _____ 6 _____

VISITING THE MOUSE

7 _____   8 _____   9 von miller

10 _____   11 _____   12 cooper kupp

SNAPSHOT IN TIME

Match the legendary Super Bowl moment to the game in which it took place.

1. William Perry smashes into the end zone for a meaningless touchdown   **A.** Super Bowl VII

2. Garo Yepremian throws a pick-six off a blocked field goal   **B.** Super Bowl XXII

3. David Tyree traps a pass against his helmet   **C.** Super Bowl XLII

4. James Harrison intercepts a pass and takes it 99 yards for a touchdown   **D.** Super Bowl XLIV

5. Lynn Swann hauls in an acrobatic catch off a deflection   **E.** Super Bowl XXI

6. The Saints spring a surprise onside kick to open the second half   **F.** Super Bowl XX

7. Leon Lett gets a bit too cocky and is run down by Don Beebe   **G.** Super Bowl LII

8. Timmy Smith remains the only player to rush for 200 yards in a Super Bowl   **H.** Super Bowl XLIII

9. The Philly Special is introduced to the world   **I.** Super Bowl XXVII

10. The lights go out in the Superdome in the middle of the Super Bowl   **J.** Super Bowl XXIX

11. Phil Simms dissects the defense for a record 88-percent completion percentage   **K.** Super Bowl XLVII

12. Steve Young breaks Joe Montana's record with his sixth touchdown pass   **L.** Super Bowl X

FIND THE TROPHY

We all know what the Lombardi Trophy looks like, correct?

A

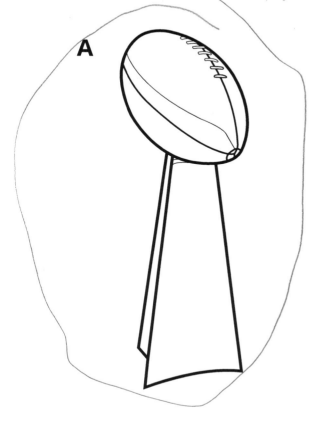

B

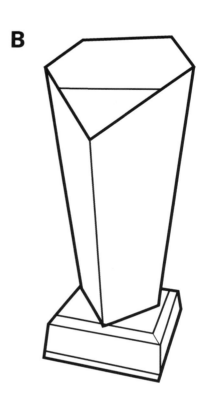

C

D

SO CLOSE CLUB

History remembers the champions, but this one is about those who were almost champions.

1. It isn't easy to get back to the Super Bowl after losing it the previous year, but it's even harder to get back to the game then fall short again. Who was the first team to lose consecutive Super Bowls?

A. Miami Dolphins   **B.** Minnesota Vikings   **C.** Dallas Cowboys   **D.** Oakland Raiders

2. Six teams had their chances to repeat as champions thwarted in the Super Bowl the following year. Which franchise was not one of those teams to lose in the Super Bowl the year after emerging victorious?

A. Green Bay Packers   **B.** Dallas Cowboys   **C.** Pittsburgh Steelers   **D.** Washington

3. Which franchise was on the losing end of the biggest blowout in Super Bowl history thanks to Joe Montana and the San Francisco 49ers?

A. Miami Dolphins   **B.** San Diego Chargers   **C.** Cincinnati Bengals   **D.** Denver Broncos

4. Everyone remembers the 1972 Miami Dolphins as the only perfect team in NFL history, but who did they beat in the Super Bowl that season to cap off the unbeaten year?

A. Washington Redskins   **B.** Dallas Cowboys   **C.** Baltimore Colts   **D.** Chicago Bears

5. How much time did Joe Montana leave the Cincinnati Bengals in Super Bowl XXIII after marching down the field on the game-winning drive in the fourth quarter?

A. 54 seconds   **B.** 44 seconds   **C.** 34 seconds   **D.** 24 seconds

6. The Buffalo Bills had a chance to win Super Bowl XXV, but the infamous "Wide Right" kick from Scott Norwood sailed wide from how many yards out in the final seconds?

A. 47 yards   **B.** 44 yards   **C.** 37 yards   **D.** 33 yards

7. Which Tennessee Titans receiver futilely stretched for the goal line in Super Bowl XXXIV on the final play of the game?

A. Isaac Byrd   **B.** Kevin Dyson   **C.** Frank Wycheck   **D.** Yancey Thigpen

8. Super Bowl XLI got off to a roaring start for the Chicago Bears when which electric playmaker ran the opening kickoff back for a 92-yard score?

A. Adrian Peterson   **B.** Charles Tillman   **C.** Chris Harris   **D.** Devin Hester

9. Russell Wilson was trying to connect with Ricardo Lockette, but instead had his goal-line pass intercepted by whom to seal a Super Bowl XLIX defeat?

A. Patrick Chung   **B.** Darrelle Revis   **C.** Devin McCourty   **D.** Malcolm Butler

10. Atlanta Falcons fans will undoubtedly remember Super Bowl LI for the team's inability to hold onto a 28-3 lead. However, who did not score one of the touchdowns that helped stake the Falcons to that advantage?

A. Austin Hooper   **B.** Tevin Coleman   **C.** Julio Jones   **D.** Devonta Freeman

Records
INCREDIBLE MOMENTS

Some of the hardest records to break in the NFL are the single-game marks because it requires one day of pure brilliance from the players. Can you remember some of the details around the best individual performances of all-time?

1. In November 1929, this Chicago Cardinals star scored six touchdowns, then added four extra points for good measure, against the crosstown rival Chicago Bears to set the NFL record with 40 points in a game.

A. Ernie Nevers   **B.** Chuck Kassel   **C.** Mickey MacDonnell   **D.** Cobb Rooney

2. Only one player in NFL history has gained 400 combined yards (rushing, receiving, interception returns, punt returns, kickoff returns and fumble returns) in a single game. It happened in 1995 for this Denver Broncos offensive weapon.

A. Anthony Miller   **B.** Terrell Davis   **C.** Aaron Craver   **D.** Glyn Milburn

3. Four quarterbacks share the record for most consecutive completions, but only two were able to string 25 straight completions together in the same game. They did it a month apart in which legendary season that also included a third quarterback completing 25 consecutive passes over the course of two games?

A. 2016   **B.** 2017   **C.** 2018   **D.** 2019

4. One of the longest records still standing is Sid Luckman's seven touchdown passes against the New York Giants in 1943. It has been tied, however, by seven different quarterbacks. Which of these passers has not tied Luckman's record?

A. Drew Brees   **B.** Peyton Manning   **C.** Y.A. Tittle   **D.** Tom Brady

5. In 2007, Adrian Peterson averaged nearly 10 yards per carry when he ran the ball 30 times for 296 yards and three scores to lead the Minnesota Vikings to a win over which AFC opponent?

A. Kansas City Chiefs   **B.** San Diego Chargers   **C.** Indianapolis Colts   **D.** Miami Dolphins

6. Who caught a record 21 passes in a 2009 game against the Indianapolis Colts, yet amassed just 200 yards and two scores in a loss?

A. Brandon Marshall   **B.** Wes Welker   **C.** Steve Smith   **D.** Hines Ward

7. Calvin Johnson holds the regulation-record for most receiving yards in a game, but this former Rams wideout holds the overall record with 336 yards and the game-tying score in an eventual overtime win over the Saints.

A. Elroy Hirsch   **B.** Isaac Bruce   **C.** Flipper Anderson   **D.** Torry Holt

8. Derrick Thomas was a nightmare for which Seahawks quarterback who he sacked seven times to set the record for most sacks in a game?

A. Rick Mirer   **B.** Dave Kreig   **C.** Stan Gelbaugh   **D.** Jim Zorn

9. Rob Bironas holds the record for most field goals made in a game when he kicked eight through the uprights for the Titans in a 2007 win over the Texans. The record-breaking kick was a game-winner on the final play from how far?

A. 29 yards   **B.** 35 yards   **C.** 42 yards   **D.** 51 yards

10. There are a handful of players who have successfully returned two kickoffs for a touchdown in the same game. However, this dynamic return man never accomplished the feat.

A. Devin Hester   **B.** Josh Cribbs   **C.** Ted Ginn Jr.   **D.** Dante Hall

INCREDIBLE TEAMS

It's not just the individuals who deserve the spotlight in the record books. Football is a team game, so it takes all 11 players working together on each side of the ball to win a championship. Can you match the franchise to which NFL team record they hold? Note: Some teams may be the answer to multiple questions, and not all teams will be used.

1. Most consecutive road games won	_____
2. Most points scored in a season	_____
3. Most penalized team in a season	_____
4. Most sacks allowed in a season	_____
5. Most consecutive games lost	_____
6. Most two-point conversions in a game	_____
7. Most first downs in a game	_____
8. Most points scored in a game	_____
9. Most interceptions in a season	_____
10. Fewest rushing attempts in a game	_____
11. Most sacks in a season	_____
12. Most rushing yards in a season	_____
13. Most safeties scored in a game	_____
14. Most kickoff return touchdowns allowed in a season	_____
15. Fewest fumbles in a season	

A. Rams
B. Eagles
C. Colts
D. Packers
E. Broncos
F. 49ers
G. Patriots
H. Chargers
I. Ravens
J. Buccaneers
K. Steelers
L. Saints
M. Commanders
N. Bears
O. Giants
P. Jaguars
Q. Raiders
R. Dolphins

RECORD SCRATCHING

There are some records that may never be broken thanks to evolutions in the sport. Injuries and rest make someone catching Brett Favre's ironman streak doubtful, while the average NFL career is short enough that no one may ever touch George Blanda's 26 NFL seasons. This quiz looks at some of the more unbreakable records and asks you just how high the standard is set.

1. Morten Andersen's record for most games played: 375 games

MORE   LESS

2. LaDanian Tomlinson's record for most points in a season: 190 points

MORE   LESS

3. Emmitt Smith's record for most career rushing attempts: 4,400 rushes

MORE   LESS

4. Matthew Stafford's record for most passing attempts in a season: 700 attempts

MORE   LESS

5. Barry Sanders' record for consecutive 100-yard rushing games: 16 games

MORE   LESS

6. Brett Favre's record for most career interceptions thrown: 340 interceptions

MORE   LESS

7. Calvin Johnson's record for most receiving yards in a season: 2,000 yards

MORE   LESS

8. Warren Moon's record for total fumble recoveries: 50 fumbles recovered

MORE   LESS

9. Reggie White's record for consecutive seasons with at least 10 sacks: 10 years

MORE   LESS

10. Chris Jones' record for most consecutive games with a sack: 10 games

MORE   LESS

YOU SPIN ME RIGHT ROUND

The beauty of records is that they are meant to be broken, and oftentimes that means we forget about those who lost the record. Not anymore. We'll have you match the person who holds the record with whose record they ended up breaking.

1. Adam Vinatieri's record for career points

A. Gary Andersen   **B.** Morten Andersen   **C.** George Blanda

2. Adrian Peterson's record for rushing yards in a game

A. Gale Sayers   **B.** Eric Dickerson   **C.** Jamal Lewis

3. Larry Johnson's record for most rushing attempts in a season

A. James Wilder   **B.** Emmitt Smith   **C.** Jamal Anderson

4. Tom Brady's record for most completions in a season

A. Tom Brady   **B.** Peyton Manning   **C.** Drew Brees

5. Justin Herbert's record for touchdown passes as a rookie

A. Baker Mayfield   **B.** Russell Wilson   **C.** Peyton Manning

6. Peyton Manning's record for passing yards in a season

A. Drew Brees   **B.** Tom Brady   **C.** Dan Marino

7. Randy Moss' record for most touchdown catches in a season

A. Terrell Owens   **B.** Jerry Rice   **C.** Marvin Harrison

8. Jason Taylor's record for most career fumbles returned for a touchdown

A. Jessie Tuggle   **B.** Derrick Thomas   **C.** Mike Singletary

9. Derrick Thomas' record for most sacks in a game

A. John Randle   **B.** Fred Dean   **C.** Reggie White

10. Chris Johnson's record for most yards from scrimmage in a season.

A. Walter Payton   **B.** Marshall Faulk   **C.** Eric Dickerson

SIMPLY THE BEST

There are certain records that have proven to be unbreakable in the Super Bowl era. Some of them are due to the changes in the sport that make holding a team to -53 passing yards nearly impossible in the modern era. However, some of the all-time greats are still holding onto their records more than half a century later, and those are the players and teams we honor with this quiz. Your job is to simply tell us who holds these seemingly unbreakable records that have stood since before the Super Bowl era.

1. 554 passing yards in a single game

A. Norm Van Brocklin   **B.** Sammy Baugh   **C.** Y.A. Tittle

2. 8.63 yards per completion in a career

A. Sid Luckman   **B.** Tommy O'Connell   **C.** Otto Graham

3. 42 interceptions thrown in a season

A. Jim Hardy   **B.** George Blanda   **C.** Frank Tripucka

4. 1,473 receiving yards as a rookie

A. Lance Alworth   **B.** Bill Groman   **C.** Don Hutson

5. 14 interceptions in a season

A. Jack Butler   **B.** Emlen Tunnell   **C.** Dick Lane

6. 27 straight games without a loss

A. Canton Bulldogs   **B.** Green Bay Packers   **C.** Chicago Bears

7. 426 rushing yards in a game

A. New York Giants   **B.** Chicago Bears   **C.** Detroit Lions

8. 37 combined penalties in a game

A. Green Bay vs. Detroit   **B.** Cleveland vs. Chicago   **C.** New York vs. Washington

9. 36 rushing touchdowns allowed

A. Oakland Raiders   **B.** Houston Oilers   **C.** Buffalo Bills

10. 66 takeaways in a season

A. San Diego Chargers   **B.** San Francisco 49ers   **C.** Dallas Cowboys

Hall of Fame
BUST IT OUT

One of the coolest parts of Hall of Fame weekend is the unveiling of the official Hall of Fame busts. Can you name these Hall of Famers by photos of their busts?

1 _Jhon madden_

2 _____

3 _____

4 _Mhiclay strahan_

5 _____

BUST IT OUT

6 JerryJones

7 _____

8 _____

9 Jerome Bettis

GO LONG

Some of the most iconic names in the sport's history have played quarterback. You could probably name quite a few of the 32 quarterbacks inducted into the Hall of Fame so far, but how much do you actually know about these signal callers?

1. Often forgotten in the conversation of great NFL quarterbacks, Otto Graham led which team to 10 straight title games, winning three NFL championships along the way?

Cleveland Browns	S	Canton Bulldogs	J

2. Bart Starr was an underappreciated quarterback as well, but he certainly was acknowledged when he was named the Super Bowl MVP of which Packers' victory?

Super Bowl I	E	Super Bowl II	U	Both	A

3. In which Canadian city did Warren Moon prove everyone wrong before signing with the Houston Oilers in 1984?

Montreal	H	Edmonton	M

4. What is Steve Young's legal first name?

Jon	M	Steven	N

5. Roger Staubach was able to forgo his mandatory service with the Navy after winning the Heisman Trophy.

FACT	T	FICTION	Y

6. How many times did John Elway fall short in the Super Bowl before he finally was able to hoist the Lombardi Trophy?

3	B	4	L

7. How many games long was Brett Favre's record streak of consecutive starts?

299	A	301	O

8. To which team was Fran Tarkenton traded by the Minnesota Vikings in 1967 before they re-acquired him five years later from the same franchise?

Los Angeles Rams	N	New York Giants	U

9. Johnny Unitas was not drafted by the Colts, rather he was drafted by this franchise, his hometown team, before being cut before throwing a single pass.

Pittsburgh Steelers	G	Washington Redskins	I

10. Which Hall of Fame quarterback was given the Pete Rozelle Radio-Television Award for his work as a broadcaster on HBO's Inside the NFL?

Phil Simms	E	Len Dawson	H	Terry Bradshaw	A

What is the oldest NFL franchise still in the league?

___ ___ ___ ___ ___   ___ ___ ___ ___ ___
1   2   3   4   5   6   7   8   9   10

IN THE TRENCHES

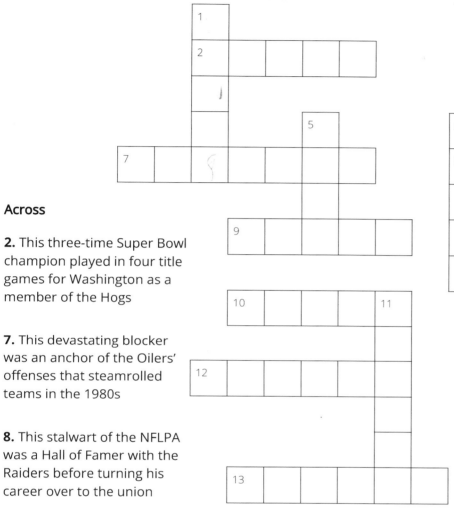

Across

2. This three-time Super Bowl champion played in four title games for Washington as a member of the Hogs

7. This devastating blocker was an anchor of the Oilers' offenses that steamrolled teams in the 1980s

8. This stalwart of the NFLPA was a Hall of Famer with the Raiders before turning his career over to the union

9. This Hall-of-Famer coached the Bengals and his beloved Packers before returning to take over at SMU after its death penalty

10. This Raiders legend came back to coach the team and his firing was one of the few times Al Davis admitted a mistake

12. He played just eight years in the NFL but all of them were with the Bears as Chicago won 10 games six times during his career

13. The first name of this Jones who was the first Seahawks offensive lineman ever elected to the Pro Bowl

Down

1. He went from being the Ravens' first-ever draft pick to being the first predominantly Baltimore player elected to the Hall of Fame

3. This Pittsburgh Steelers anchor was one of the centers on the 1990s All-Decade Team

4. No injury was going to keep this Packers legend from paving the way for five of the team's NFL titles

5. There was no doubting this tackle's greatness from being the top pick to being part of the Greatest Show on Turf

6. This Bengals trailblazer was named an All-Pro 11 straight seasons and kept the pocket clean for both Cincinnati teams that won AFC titles in the 1980s

11. This Dolphins legend played a pretty "big" part of the team's success in the 1970s despite going undrafted

PICK SIX

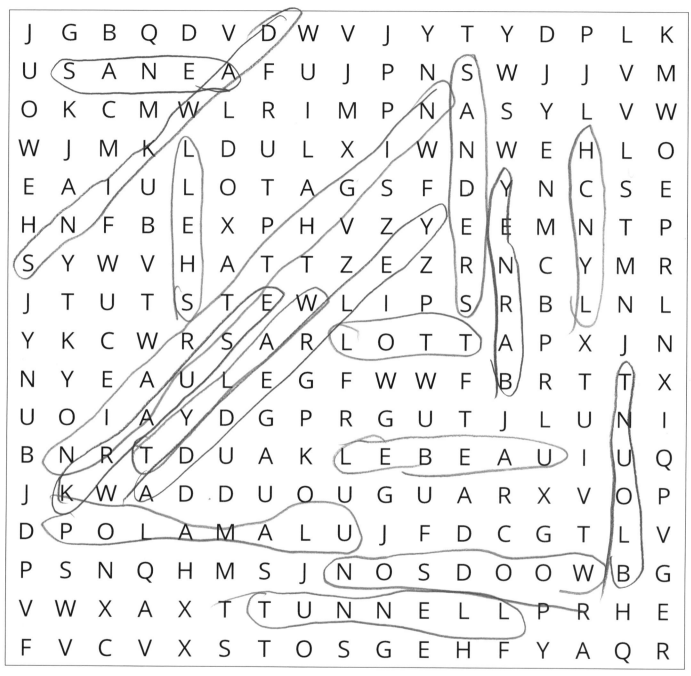

J G B Q D V D W V J Y T Y D P L K
U S A N E A F U J P N S W J J V M
O K C M W L R I M P N A S Y L V W
W J M K L D U L X I W N W E H L O
E A I U L O T A G S F D Y N C S E
H N F B E X P H V Z Y E E M N T P
S Y W V H A T T Z E Z R N C Y M R
J T U T S T E W L I P S R B L N L
Y K C W R S A R L O T T A P X J N
N Y E A U L E G F W W F B R T X X
U O I A Y D G P R G U T J L U N I
B N R T D U A K L E B E A U I U Q
J K W A D D U O U G U A R X V O P
D P O L A M A L U J F D C G T V P
P S N Q H M S J N O S D O O W B G
V W X A X T T U N N E L L P R H E
F V C V X S T O S G E H F Y A Q R

Woodson   Lott
Ty Law   LeBeau
Tunnell   Kraus
Shell   Dawkins
Sanders   Blount
Polamalu   Barney
Night Train   Aenas
Lynch   Adderley

IN A HURRY

Can you unscramble the names of these Hall of Fame pass rushers before they come to sack you?

1. EILVN TEHEBA — *Elvin Bethea*

2. OEJ REENEG — *Joe Greene*

3. UYMAELULABRC —

4. AHCESRL EHAYL — *Charles Haley*

5. NMEIRL NSOLE — *merlin olsen*

6. GIGREE EWITH — *Reggie White*

7. JKAC OUOOYGNDLB — *Jack Youngblood*

8. CAJK MAH — *Jack Ham*

9. KICN OOTICBNUNI — *nick Buoniconti*

10. YAHRR CONASR — *Harry carson*

11. KCJA LTBREAM — *Jack Lambert*

12. ENLEACRW LTRAOY — *Lawrence taylor*

CONCLUSION

Congratulations on reaching the end of the puzzles, we certainly hope you enjoyed yourself. If we've done our job correctly then you've learned something new but also tested yourself with some original information about the NFL. This book spanned it all, from the very basics of football to the best players to ever play in the pros. We covered the history of all 32 NFL franchises and almost every notable player who has ended up in Canton, Ohio as well.

No one could have predicted just how popular the NFL would become when it was first established. Certainly Walter Camp and the early pioneers of the sport could not have predicted football would become the predominant sport in the United States the way it has over the past five decades. That is a credit to many of the names we mentioned in this book, but also a credit to fans like you who have stuck with the sport. The NFL is a constantly evolving league, and this book will look much different in five or 10 years down the line.

But for right now, we hope you enjoyed your foray into our puzzles, and be sure to check out our other puzzle books on a wide variety of sports.

SOLUTIONS

THE ORIGIN STORY (PAGE 3)

1) Fact; **2)** Fiction, the first completely professional franchise was in 1896; **3)** Fact; **4)** Fact, Matthewson played for the Pittsburgh Stars; **5)** Fiction, the forward pass was legalized in 1906, seven years before Thorpe's debut; **6)** Fiction, in 1898, the touchdown's value increased to five points and it wasn't until 1904 when the field goal was diminished from five points to four. The scoring system we know today was established in 1909 when the field goal became worth three points, then in 1912 when the touchdown became six points; **7)** Fiction; **8)** Fact; **9)** Fiction, The Lions played the Bears on Thanksgiving Day 1934; CARDINALS

FLAG ON THE PLAY (PAGE 4)

Maze Results

BE THE REF (PAGE 5)

1) Safety; **2)** Holding; **3)** Intentional Grounding; **4)** First Down; **5)** Ineligible Player Downfield; **6)** Loss of Down; **7)** Illegal Substitution/Too Many Men on the Field; **8)** Illegal Contact; **9)** Illegal Use of Hands; **10)** Delay of Game; **11)** Illegal Touching; **12)** Pass Interference

READY POSITION (PAGE 6)

1) Center; **2)** Halfback; **3)** Offensive Tackle; **4)** Wide Receiver; **5)** Fullback; **6)** Tight End; **7)** Quarterback; **8)** Offensive Guard; **9)** Defensive End; **10)** Defensive Tackle; **11)** Outside Linebacker; **12)** Inside Linebacker; **13)** Cornerback; **14)** Safety

FIND THE TERM (PAGE 7)

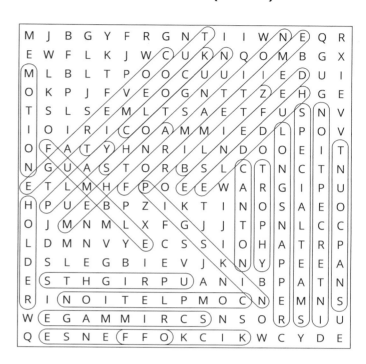

WHAT'S IN A NAME? (PAGE 8)

Across: 2) Packers; **5)** Chiefs; **8)** Niners; **11)** Patriots; **12)** Giants; **13)** Cardinals; **Down: 1)** Browns; **3)** Steelers; **4)** Vikings; **6)** Ravens; **7)** Jets; **9)** Saints; **10)** Rams;

THE RAINBOW CONNECTION (PAGE 9)

1) Texans; **2)** Chargers; **3)** Lions; **4)** Dolphins; **5)** Eagles; **6)** Saints; **7)** Buccaneers; **8)** Seahawks; **9)** Rams

LOGO DESCRIPTION (PAGE 9)

1) L; **2)** C; **3)** P; **4)** D; **5)** O; **6)** G; **7)** F; **8)** M; **9)** B; **10)** K; **11)** E; **12)** N; **13)** H; **14)** I; **15)** J; **16)** A

SOLUTIONS

LARGE AND IN CHARGE (PAGE 11)

1) B; **2)** C; **3)** A; **4)** E; **5)** C; **6)** B;
7) D; **8)** E; **9)** B; **10)** D

NOT FOR LONG LEAGUE (PAGE 12)

1) D; **2)** B; **3)** A; **4)** C; **5)** A; **6)** B;
7) B; **8)** A; **9)** D; **10)** C

EXPANDING THE FOOTPRINT (PAGE 13)

1) Fiction, the Packers joined the league in 1921, four years before the Giants;
2) Fact; **3)** Fact; **4)** Fiction, the Falcons joined in 1966 and the Saints in 1967;
5) Fiction, the Dolphins didn't join the AFL until 1966; **6)** Fiction, the Buccaneers and Seahawks joined in 1976; **7)** Fact, when the Browns were reinstated in 1999, the Ravens were designated an expansion franchise; **8)** Fiction, they joined in 1995;
9) Fact; **10)** Fact; **11)** Fiction, the 49ers and Rams both joined from other leagues;
12) Fact; INDIANAPOLIS

THE MOVING COMPANY (PAGE 14)

1) Commanders; **2)** Rams; **3)** Chargers;
4) Cardinals; **5)** Colts; **6)** Raiders;
7) Titans; **8)** Ravens

X'S AND O'S (PAGE 15)

1) Marv Levy; **2)** Paul Brown; **3)** Curly Lambeau;
4) Tom Landry; **5)** Bill Walsh; **6)** Vince Lombardi;
7) Chuck Noll; **8)** Bud Grant; **9)** John Madden;
10) Bill Parcells; **11)** Don Shula; **12)** Hank Stram;
13) Bill Belichick; **14)** Tom Flores;
15) George Halas

ROAMING THE SIDELINES (PAGE 16)

1) Don Shula; **2)** Bill Parcells; **3)** Herm Edwards;
4) Vince Lombardi; **5)** Dennis Green; **6)** George Halas; **7)** Bum Phillips; **8)** Jim Mora; **9)** Marv Levy;
10) Bill Belichick

THE FOOLISH CLUB (PAGE 17)

1) E; **2)** G; **3)** D; **4)** A; **5)** C; **6)** F; **7)** H; **8)** B

RAINING MONEY (PAGE 17)

1) More; **2)** Less; **3)** More; **4)** More; **5)** More;
6) Less; **7)** Less; **8)** More; **9)** More; **10)** Less

THAT'S WHAT THEY CALL ME (PAGE 18)

1) B; **2)** D; **3)** C; **4)** C; **5)** A; **6)** D;
7) A; **8)** A; **9)** B; **10)** D

SOLUTIONS

LEGENDS OF THE GAME (PAGE 19)

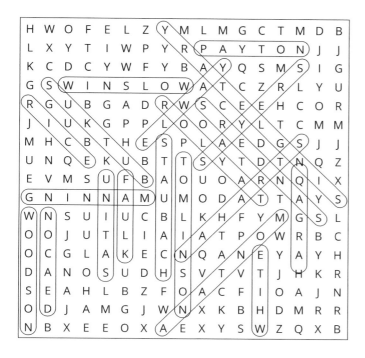

AFC EAST HUNT (PAGE 23)

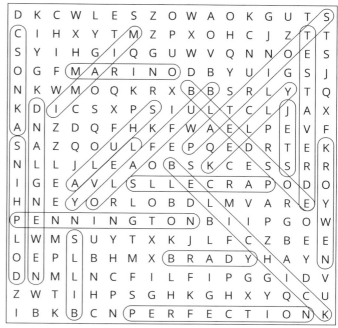

THE SPECIAL TEAM (PAGE 20)

1) Fiction, both Justin Tucker and Harrison Butker enter the 2022 NFL season with at least 90-percent success rates; **2)** Fact; **3)** Fact; **4)** Fiction, Gary Andersen in 1998 (35 attempts) and Mike Vanderjagt in 2003 (37) made every field goal; **5)** Fiction, Brian Mitchell holds the record at more than 14,000 kickoff return yards; **6)** Fact; **7)** Fiction, Harry Newsome set the record in 1988; **8)** Fact; **9)** Fiction, George Blanda made 943 extra points, 69 more than Vinatieri; **10)** Fact, Vinatieri retired with 599 makes; **11)** Fact; JEFF FEAGLES

KNOW YOUR DRAFT (PAGE 24)

AFC East: 1) A; **2)** C; **3)** B; **4)** D; **5)** C; **6)** B; **7)** A; **8)** A; **9)** B; **10)** D; **11)** C; **12)** A

BUFFALO BILLS JERSEY MATH (PAGE 25)

1) Kyle Williams, 95=83+12; **2)** Fred Smerlas, 76=5*15+1; **3)** Joe Cribbs, 20=42-22; **4)** Cornelius Bennett, 97=80+17; **5)** Steve Tasker, 89=100-11; **6)** Kent Hull, 67=90-23; **7)** 84, 84=[8+34]*2; **8)** Ruben Brown, 79=27*3-2; **9)** Mark Kelso, 38=94-56; **10)** Jairus Byrd, 31=51-20

SOLUTIONS

HISTORY OF THE BUFFALO BILLS (PAGE 26)

1) D; **2)** A; **3)** B; **4)** B; **5)** A; **6)** C;
7) D; **8)** C; **9)** A; **10)** B

MIAMI DOLPHINS 3 & OUT (PAGE 27)

1) C; **2)** A; **3)** D; **4)** D; **5)** A; **6)** A;
7) C; **8)** C; **9)** A; **10)** B

HISTORY OF THE MIAMI DOLPHINS (PAGE 28)

1) A; **2)** B; **3)** D; **4)** B; **5)** C; **6)** A;
7) D; **8)** B; **9)** B; **10)** C

NEW YORK JETS ALMA MATERS (PAGE 29)

1) K; **2)** M; **3)** F; **4)** L; **5)** B; **6)** C; **7)** I; **8)** G; **9)** J;
10) D; **11)** H; **12)** E; **13)** N; **14)** O; **15)** A

HISTORY OF THE NEW YORK JETS (PAGE 30)

1) C; **2)** A; **3)** C; **4)** D; **5)** D; **6)** B;
7) B; **8)** C; **9)** B; **10)** A

NEW ENGLAND PATRIOTS FAST FACTS (PAGE 31)

Across: 4) Foxborough; **6)** Rush;
9) Martin; **11)** Cappelletti; **12)** Eason;
Down: 1) Fryar; **2)** Houston;
3) Sullivan; **5)** Hannah; **7)** Slater;
8) Pat; **10)** Gilmore

HISTORY OF THE NEW ENGLAND PATRIOTS (PAGE 32)

1) B; **2)** A; **3)** D; **4)** C; **5)** A; **6)** A;
7) B; **8)** D; **9)** D; **10)** A

AFC NORTH HUNT (PAGE 33)

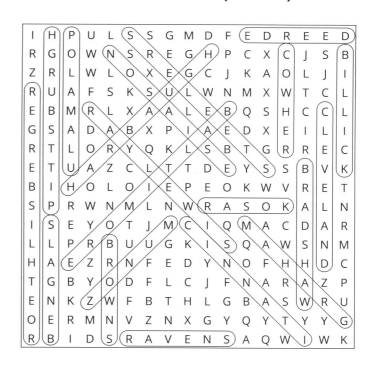

SOLUTIONS

KNOW YOUR DRAFT (PAGE 34)

AFC North: 1) A; **2)** B; **3)** D; **4)** A; **5)** B; **6)** B;
7) D; **8)** C; **9)** B; **10)** D; **11)** A; **12)** C

CINCINNATI BENGALS FAST FACTS (PAGE 35)

Across: 2) Chase; **4)** Gregg; **8)** Fifty Four;
9) Central; **10)** Montoya; **11)** Munoz; **12)** Stofa;
Down: 1) Freezer Bowl; **3)** Pete; **5)** Ochocinco;
6) Cinergy; **7)** Johnson

HISTORY OF THE CINCINNATI BENGALS (PAGE 36)

1) D; **2)** B; **3)** C; **4)** A; **5)** A; **6)** C;
7) B; **8)** D; **9)** D; **10)** A

CLEVELAND BROWNS 3 & OUT (PAGE 37)

1) C; **2)** D; **3)** B; **4)** A; **5)** B; **6)** C;
7) A; **8)** A; **9)** B; **10)** D

HISTORY OF THE CLEVELAND BROWNS (PAGE 38)

1) A; **2)** B; **3)** D; **4)** D; **5)** C; **6)** B;
7) A; **8)** C; **9)** C; **10)** B

BALTIMORE RAVENS JERSEY MATH (PAGE 39)

1) Matt Birk, 77=57+20; **2)** Sam Koch, 4=88/22;
3) Deion Sanders, 37=89-52; **4)** 40, 40=5*8;
5) Calais Campbell, 93=31*3;
6) Jonathan Ogden, 75=81-6; **7)** Shannon
Sharpe, 82=8+74; **8)** Haloti Ngata, 92=34+58;
9) Randall Cunningham, 1=86-85;
10) Jeff Blake, 11=55/5

HISTORY OF THE BALTIMORE RAVENS (PAGE 40)

1) C; **2)** B; **3)** D; **4)** B; **5)** A; **6)** A;
7) C; **8)** B; **9)** D; **10)** D

PITTSBURGH STEELERS ALMA MATERS (PAGE 41)

1) J; **2)** N; **3)** L; **4)** M; **5)** O; **6)** E; **7)** H; **8)** K; **9)** C;
10) G; **11)** I; **12)** F; **13)** A; **14)** B; **15)** D

HISTORY OF THE PITTSBURGH STEELERS (PAGE 42)

1) C; **2)** A; **3)** B; **4)** C; **5)** B; **6)** B;
7) D; **8)** D; **9)** A; **10)** C

SOLUTIONS

AFC SOUTH HUNT (PAGE 43)

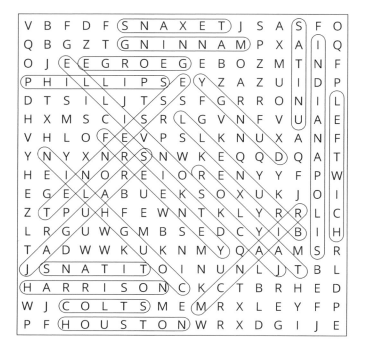

KNOW YOUR DRAFT (PAGE 44)

AFC South: 1) B; **2)** B; **3)** A; **4)** C; **5)** A; **6)** D;
7) D; **8)** C; **9)** B; **10)** C; **11)** D; **12)** B

INDIANAPOLIS COLTS 3 & OUT (PAGE 45)

1) B; **2)** A; **3)** C; **4)** C; **5)** D; **6)** A;
7) C; **8)** D; **9)** A; **10)** C

HISTORY OF THE INDIANAPOLIS COLTS (PAGE 46)

1) B; **2)** D; **3)** A; **4)** D; **5)** C; **6)** B;
7) C; **8)** A; **9)** A; **10)** D

JACKSONVILLE JAGUARS JERSEY MATH (PAGE 47)

1) Blake Bortles, 5=30-25; **2)** Marcus Stroud,
99=90+9; **3)** Allen Robinson, 15=8+7;
4) Hardy Nickerson, 56=8*7; **5)** Keenan
McCardell, 87=16+71; **6)** 60, 60=28+32;
7) Josh Allen, 41=51-10; **8)** 47, 47=20+27;
9) John Henderson, 98=97+1; **10)** Jimmy Smith,
82=7+8+11+16+10+12+11+7

HISTORY OF THE JACKSONVILLE JAGUARS (PAGE 48)

1) C; **2)** C; **3)** B; **4)** A; **5)** D; **6)** D;
7) B; **8)** C; **9)** A; **10)** C

HOUSTON TEXANS FAST FACTS (PAGE 49)

Across: 3) Kubiak; **7)** Capers; **8)** McNair;
11) Boselli; **12)** Johnson;
Down: 1) O'Brien; **2)** Yates;
4) Schaub; **5)** Mathis; **6)** Carr;
9) Cushing; **10)** Clowney

SOLUTIONS

HISTORY OF THE HOUSTON TEXANS (PAGE 50)

1) A; **2)** B; **3)** B; **4)** D; **5)** C; **6)** C;
7) A; **8)** A; **9)** C; **10)** B

KNOW YOUR DRAFT (PAGE 53)

AFC West: 1) B; **2)** A; **3)** C; **4)** C; **5)** D; **6)** C;
7) A; **8)** A; **9)** B; **10)** D; **11)** D; **12)** B

TENNESSEE TITANS ALMA MATERS (PAGE 51)

1) F; **2)** I; **3)** E; **4)** K; **5)** J; **6)** N; **7)** B; **8)** L; **9)** H;
10) O; **11)** D; **12)** A; **13)** G; **14)** C; **15)** M

DENVER BRONCOS 3 & OUT (PAGE 54)

1) A; **2)** B; **3)** C; **4)** D; **5)** B; **6)** A;
7) A; **8)** C; **9)** B; **10)** D

HISTORY OF THE TENNESSEE TITANS (PAGE 51)

1) C; **2)** A; **3)** B; **4)** B; **5)** D; **6)** A;
7) B; **8)** D; **9)** C; **10)** D

HISTORY OF THE DENVER BRONCOS (PAGE 55)

1) A; **2)** C; **3)** B; **4)** C; **5)** D; **6)** A;
7) D; **8)** B; **9)** B; **10)** C

AFC WEST HUNT (PAGE 52)

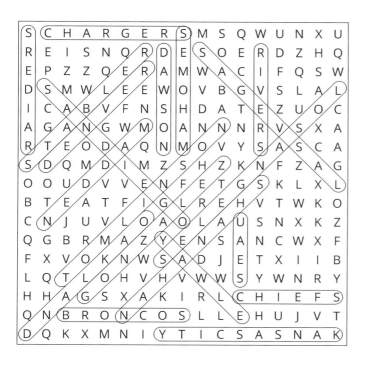

LOS ANGELES CHARGERS JERSEY MATH (PAGE 56)

1) Kellen Winslow, 80=5*16; **2)** Shawne Merriman, 56=20+36; **3)** Junior Seau, 55=14+41; **4)** John Carney, 3=30/10; **5)** Fred Dean, 71=10+61; **6)** Walt Sweeney, 78=6*13; **7)** Philip Rivers, 17=91-74; **8)** 37, 37=18+19; **9)** 64, 64=85-21; **10)** Wes Chandler, 89-1=43+45

HISTORY OF THE LOS ANGELES CHARGERS (PAGE 57)

1) D; **2)** C; **3)** C; **4)** A; **5)** B; **6)** B;
7) A; **8)** D; **9)** D; **10)** A

SOLUTIONS

KANSAS CITY CHIEFS FAST FACTS (PAGE 58)

Across: 5) Thomas; **7)** Buchanan; **8)** Lanier;
9) Dallas; **11)** Five; **12)** Fisher;

Down: 1) Holmes; **2)** Steadman; **3)** Stram;
4) Taylor; **6)** Municipal; **10)** Stenerud

HISTORY OF THE KANSAS CITY CHIEFS (PAGE 59)

1) D; **2)** B; **3)** A; **4)** B; **5)** D; **6)** A;
7) C; **8)** C; **9)** A; **10)** B

LAS VEGAS RAIDERS ALMA MATERS (PAGE 60)

1) I; **2)** G; **3)** B; **4)** L; **5)** J; **6)** D; **7)** F; **8)** C; **9)** A;
10) E; **11)** K; **12)** N; **13)** M; **14)** O; **15)** H

HISTORY OF THE LAS VEGAS RAIDERS (PAGE 61)

1) B; **2)** A; **3)** C; **4)** D; **5)** D; **6)** B;
7) D; **8)** C; **9)** C; **10)** B

NFC EAST HUNT (PAGE 63)

KNOW YOUR DRAFT (PAGE 64)

NFC East: 1) D; **2)** A; **3)** B; **4)** A; **5)** C; **6)** D;
7) A; **8)** D; **9)** C; **10)** B; **11)** C; **12)** B

WASHINGTON COMMANDERS ALMA MATERS (PAGE 65)

1) N; **2)** D; **3)** J; **4)** H; **5)** C; **6)** O; **7)** A; **8)** B; **9)** L;
10) F; **11)** M; **12)** K; **13)** G; **14)** E; **15)** I

HISTORY OF THE WASHINGTON COMMANDERS (PAGE 66)

1) A; **2)** C; **3)** B; **4)** B; **5)** D; **6)** D;
7) A; **8)** C; **9)** C; **10)** B

SOLUTIONS

DALLAS COWBOYS FAST FACTS (PAGE 67)

Across: 4) Murchison; **6)** Schramm;
10) Cotton Bowl; **11)** Adderley; **12)** Howley;
Down: 1) Packers; **2)** Landry;
3) Murray; **5)** Johnson; **7)** Oxnard;
8) Too Tall; **9)** Arlington

NEW YORK GIANTS JERSEY MATH (PAGE 71)

1) Jim Katcavage, 75=44+31; **2)** Joe Morrison, 40=4*10; **3)** Ward Cuff, 14=21-7; **4)** Jessie Armstead, 98=45+53; **5)** Spider Lockhard, 43=56-13; **6)** Charlie Conerly, 42=16*2+10; **7)** Ray Flaherty, 1=81-80; **8)** Michael Strahan, 92=50+27+15; **9)** 20, 20=72-52; **10)** Justin Tuck, 91=11+80

HISTORY OF THE DALLAS COWBOYS (PAGE 68)

1) D; **2)** D; **3)** C; **4)** A; **5)** B; **6)** B;
7) C; **8)** A; **9)** A; **10)** D

HISTORY OF THE NEW YORK GIANTS (PAGE 72)

1) C; **2)** B; **3)** A; **4)** B; **5)** D; **6)** A;
7) B; **8)** C; **9)** C; **10)** A

PHILADELPHIA EAGLES 3 & OUT (PAGE 69)

1) C; **2)** A; **3)** D; **4)** D; **5)** B; **6)** C;
7) D; **8)** A; **9)** A; **10)** C

NFC NORTH HUNT (PAGE 73)

HISTORY OF THE PHILADELPHIA EAGLES (PAGE 70)

1) B; **2)** A; **3)** C; **4)** D; **5)** A; **6)** A;
7) C; **8)** B; **9)** B; **10)** D

SOLUTIONS

KNOW YOUR DRAFT (PAGE 74)

NFC North: 1) C; **2)** B; **3)** D; **4)** C; **5)** D; **6)** A;
7) A; **8)** B; **9)** B; **10)** D; **11)** C; **12)** A

GREEN BAY PACKERS 3 & OUT (PAGE 79)

1) B; **2)** A; **3)** D; **4)** A; **5)** C; **6)** D;
7) B; **8)** A; **9)** C; **10)** B

CHICAGO BEARS ALMA MATERS (PAGE 75)

1) I; **2)** F; **3)** O; **4)** G; **5)** C; **6)** D; **7)** B; **8)** E; **9)** N;
10) K; **11)** H; **12)** A; **13)** M; **14)** J; **15)** L

HISTORY OF THE GREEN BAY PACKERS (PAGE 80)

1) D; **2)** A; **3)** C; **4)** C; **5)** D; **6)** B;
7) A; **8)** A; **9)** C; **10)** B

HISTORY OF THE CHICAGO BEARS (PAGE 76)

1) B; **2)** A; **3)** C; **4)** C; **5)** B; **6)** D;
7) A; **8)** D; **9)** B; **10)** B

MINNESOTA VIKINGS JERSEY MATH (PAGE 81)

1) Randy Moss, 84=8+76; **2)** Chris Doleman, 56=74-18; **3)** Jim Marshall, 70=14*3+28;
4) Korey Stringer, 77=55+22; **5)** Mick Tingelhoff, 53=26*2+1; **6)** Cris Carter, 80=69+11; **7)** John Randle, 93=65+28; **8)** Ron Yary, 73=82+1-10;
9) Randall McDaniel, 64=97-33;
10) Alan Page, 88=7+81

DETROIT LIONS FAST FACTS (PAGE 77)

Across: 2) Barney; **5)** Parker; **7)** Portsmouth;
9) Dutch; **11)** Vikings; **12)** Pontiac;
Down: 1) Paper Lion; **3)** Layne; **4)** Jones;
6) Fontes; **8)** Spielman; **10)** Hanson

HISTORY OF THE DETROIT LIONS (PAGE 78)

1) C; **2)** B; **3)** D; **4)** D; **5)** A; **6)** B;
7) D; **8)** A; **9)** C; **10)** C

HISTORY OF THE MINNESOTA VIKINGS (PAGE 82)

1) C; **2)** A; **3)** D; **4)** C; **5)** B; **6)** A;
7) A; **8)** D; **9)** C; **10)** A

SOLUTIONS

NFC SOUTH HUNT (PAGE 83)

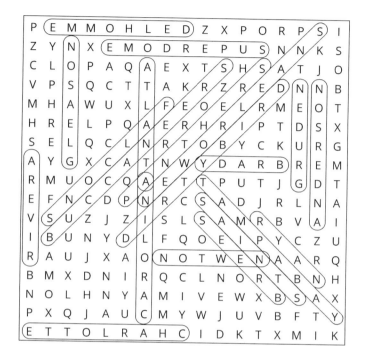

KNOW YOUR DRAFT (PAGE 84)

NFC South: 1) B; **2)** C; **3)** D; **4)** D; **5)** A; **6)** B;
7) B; **8)** C; **9)** D; **10)** A; **11)** B; **12)** A

TAMPA BAY BUCCANEERS FAST FACTS (PAGE 85)

Across: 4) Cadillac; **7)** Big Sombrero; **9)** Saints;
10) Culverhouse; **11)** Disney; **12)** Selmon;
Down: 1) Captain; **2)** McKay; **3)** Wilder;
5) Brooks; **6)** Creamsicle; **8)** Barber

HISTORY OF THE TAMPA BAY BUCCANEERS (PAGE 86)

1) A; **2)** D; **3)** D; **4)** A; **5)** C; **6)** B;
7) B; **8)** C; **9)** A; **10)** D

ATLANTA FALCONS 3 & OUT (PAGE 87)

1) B; **2)** A; **3)** D; **4)** C; **5)** A; **6)** B;
7) B; **8)** D; **9)** C; **10)** C

HISTORY OF THE ATLANTA FALCONS (PAGE 88)

1) D; **2)** C; **3)** B; **4)** A; **5)** A; **6)** B;
7) B; **8)** D; **9)** C; **10)** D

CAROLINA PANTHERS JERSEY MATH (PAGE 89)

1) Ryan Kalil, 68=34*2-1; **2)** Thomas Davis, 58=30+28; **3)** Greg Olsen, 88=22*4; **4)** Chris Gamble, 20=97-77; **5)** Josh Norman, 24=11+13; **6)** Steve Smith, 89=87+2; **7)** Shaq Thompson, 54=3*17; **8)** 7, 85/12=7 and 1/12; **9)** 31, 31=90-59; **10)** Mike Rucker, 93=70+23

SOLUTIONS

HISTORY OF THE CAROLINA PANTHERS (PAGE 90)

1) B; **2)** A; **3)** C; **4)** D; **5)** A; **6)** D; **7)** D; **8)** C; **9)** B; **10)** A

NEW ORLEANS SAINTS ALMA MATERS (PAGE 91)

1) L; **2)** D; **3)** F; **4)** G; **5)** I; **6)** N; **7)** O; **8)** A; **9)** B; **10)** C; **11)** M; **12)** K; **13)** H; **14)** J; **15)** E

HISTORY OF THE NEW ORLEANS SAINTS (PAGE 92)

1) B; **2)** C; **3)** A; **4)** A; **5)** D; **6)** C; **7)** B; **8)** D; **9)** A; **10)** A

NFC WEST HUNT (PAGE 93)

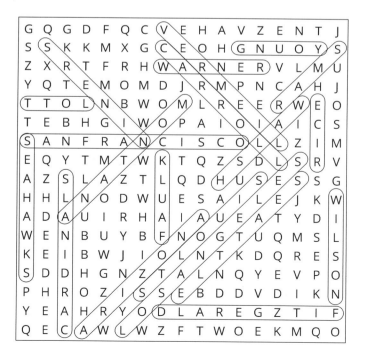

KNOW YOUR DRAFT (PAGE 94)

NFC West: 1) B; **2)** A; **3)** B; **4)** D; **5)** D; **6)** C; **7)** B; **8)** C; **9)** A; **10)** A; **11)** C; **12)** B

SAN FRANCISCO 49ERS ALMA MATERS (PAGE 95)

1) L; **2)** F; **3)** A; **4)** G; **5)** H; **6)** M; **7)** E; **8)** O; **9)** B; **10)** C; **11)** J; **12)** K; **13)** D; **14)** I; **15)** N

HISTORY OF THE SAN FRANCISCO 49ERS (PAGE 96)

1) C; **2)** A; **3)** B; **4)** D; **5)** D; **6)** B; **7)** A; **8)** A; **9)** C; **10)** B

ARIZONA CARDINALS JERSEY MATH (PAGE 97)

1) Dan Dierdorf, 72=40+32; **2)** Shawne Merriman, John David Crow, 44=16+28; **3)** Chandler Jones, 55=77-22; **4)** Ollie Matson, 33=3*11; **5)** Jim Hart, 17=47-30; **6)** Marshall Goldberg, 99=67+32; **7)** Aenas Williams, 35=36-1; **8)** Larry Fitzgerald, 11=88/8; **9)** Patrick Peterson, 21=[81+3]/4; **10)** 2, 2=58-56

SOLUTIONS

HISTORY OF THE ARIZONA CARDINALS (PAGE 98)

1) B; **2)** D; **3)** A; **4)** C; **5)** C; **6)** B;
7) D; **8)** A; **9)** A; **10)** B

LOS ANGELES RAMS FAST FACTS (PAGE 99)

Across: 2) Slater; **3)** Green;
7) Cleveland; **8)** Ellard; **10)** Frontiere;
11) Inglewood; **12)** Jackson;
Down: 1) Waterfield; **4)** Warner;
5) Rozelle; **6)** Deacon; **9)** Bezdek

HISTORY OF THE LOS ANGELES RAMS (PAGE 100)

1) D; **2)** C; **3)** B; **4)** B; **5)** A; **6)** A;
7) D; **8)** C; **9)** C; **10)** B

SEATTLE SEAHAWKS 3 & OUT (PAGE 101)

1) C; **2)** A; **3)** B; **4)** A; **5)** D; **6)** C;
7) B; **8)** B; **9)** D; **10)** A

HISTORY OF THE SEATTLE SEAHAWKS (PAGE 102)

1) A; **2)** B; **3)** D; **4)** A; **5)** C; **6)** C;
7) B; **8)** D; **9)** D; **10)** A

LOCATION, LOCATION, LOCATION (PAGE 104)

Miami 11; New Orleans 10; Los Angeles 8;
Tampa 5; Phoenix 3; Atlanta 3; Houston 3;
San Diego 3; Detroit 2; Minneapolis 2;
San Francisco 2; Indianapolis 1;
Jacksonville 1; New York City 1; Dallas 1

VISITING THE MOUSE (PAGE 105)

1) Richard Dent; **2)** Ottis Anderson;
3) Jake Scott; **4)** Mark Rypien; **5)** Larry Brown;
6) Dexter Jackson; **7)** Desmond Howard;
8) Deion Branch; **9)** Von Miller;
10) Malcolm Smith; **11)** Julian Edelman;
12) Cooper Kupp

SNAPSHOT IN TIME (PAGE 107)

1) F; **2)** A; **3)** C; **4)** H; **5)** L; **6)** D;
7) I; **8)** B; **9)** G; **10)** K; **11)** E; **12)** J

FIND THE TROPHY (PAGE 108)

The real Lombardi Trophy is A.

SOLUTIONS

SO CLOSE CLUB (PAGE 109)
1) B; **2)** C; **3)** D; **4)** A; **5)** C; **6)** A;
7) B; **8)** D; **9)** D; **10)** C

YOU SPIN ME RIGHT ROUND (PAGE 113)
1) B; **2)** C; **3)** C; **4)** C; **5)** A; **6)** A;
7) B; **8)** A; **9)** B; **10)** B

INCREDIBLE MOMENTS (PAGE 110)
1) A; **2)** D; **3)** C; **4)** D; **5)** B; **6)** A;
7) C; **8)** B; **9)** A; **10)** D

SIMPLY THE BEST (PAGE 114)
1) A; **2)** C; **3)** B; **4)** B; **5)** C; **6)** A;
7) C; **8)** B; **9)** A; **10)** A

INCREDIBLE TEAMS (PAGE 111)
1) F; **2)** E; **3)** Q; **4)** B; **5)** J; **6)** A; **7)** L; **8)** M; **9)** H;
10) J; **11)** N; **12)** I; **13)** A; **14)** K; **15)** L

BUST IT OUT (PAGE 115)
1) John Madden; **2)** Barry Sanders;
3) Brett Favre; **4)** Michael Strahan;
5) Deion Sanders; **6)** Jerry Jones;
7) Paul Tagliabue; **8)** Jerry Rice;
9) Jerome Bettis

RECORD SCRATCHING (PAGE 112)
1) Higher (382 games); **2)** Lower (186 points);
3) Higher (4,409 rushes); **4)** Higher (727
attempts in 2012); **5)** Lower (14 games);
6) Lower (336 interceptions); **7)** Lower (1,964
yards in 2012); **8)** Higher (56 recoveries);
9) Lower (9 years); **10)** Higher
(11 games in 2018)

GO LONG (PAGE 117)
1) Cleveland Browns; **2)** Both;
3) Edmonton; **4)** Jon; **5)** Fiction; **6)** 3; **7)** 299;
8) New York Giants; **9)** Pittsburgh Steelers;
10) Len Dawson; SAMMY BAUGH

SOLUTIONS

IN THE TRENCHES (PAGE 118)

Across: 2) Grimm; **7)** Munchak; **8)** Upshaw; **9)** Gregg;
10) Shell; **12)** Covert; **13)** Walter;

Down: 1) Ogden; **3)** Dawson; **4)** Kramer; **5)** Pace;
6) Munoz; **11)** Little;

PICK SIX (PAGE 119)

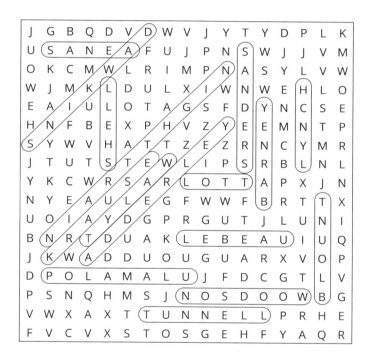

IN A HURRY (PAGE 120)

1) Elvin Bethea; **2)** Joe Greene; **3)** Charles Haley;
4) Deacon Jones; **5)** Merlin Olsen; **6)** Reggie White;
7) Jack Youngblood; **8)** Jack Ham; **9)** Nick Buoniconti;
10) Harry Carson; **11)** Jack Lambert; **12)** Lawrence Taylor

Made in the USA
Columbia, SC
12 December 2022

73542037R00078